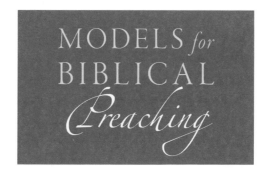

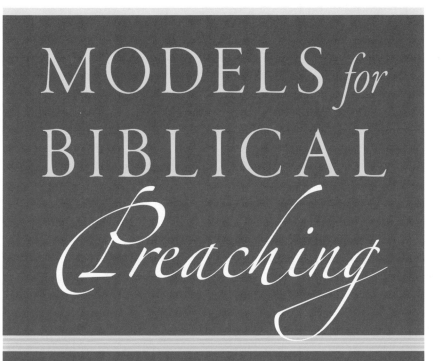

MODELS *for* BIBLICAL *Preaching*

EXPOSITORY SERMONS
FROM THE OLD TESTAMENT

EDITED BY

HADDON W. ROBINSON
AND PATRICIA BATTEN

Baker Academic
a division of Baker Publishing Group
Grand Rapids, Michigan

Published by Baker Academic
a division of Baker Publishing Group
P.O. Box 6287, Grand Rapids, MI 49516-6287
www.bakeracademic.com

Printed in the United States of America

Library of Congress Cataloging-in-Publication Data
Models for biblical preaching : expository sermons from the Old Testament / edited by Haddon W. Robinson and Patricia Batten.
    pages cm.
  Includes bibliographical references and index.
  ISBN 978-0-8010-4937-8 (pbk.)
  1. Bible. Old Testament—Sermons. 2. Preaching I. Robinson, Haddon W., editor of compilation.
  BS1151.55.M63 2014
  252—dc23   2013047468

14   15   16   17   18   19   20   7   6   5   4   3   2   1

Contents

A Word to the Reader   vii

1. Climbing Test Mountain: *Genesis 22:1–19*   1
   Bryan Wilkerson

2. How to Say God's Name: *Exodus 20:7*   23
   Eric Dokken

3. The Story of the Left-Handed Assassin and the Obese King:
   Judges 3:12–30   41
   Steve Mathewson

4. The Story of the Worship Leader Who Lost His Song:
   Psalm 73   61
   Patricia Batten

5. Sounds That Make a Noise: *Proverbs 22:1*   77
   Sid Buzzell

6. Ego Adjustment: *Ecclesiastes 3:9–15*   97
   Scott Wenig

7. Overhearing a Counseling Session: *Isaiah 43:1–3a*   113
   Ramona Spilman

8. Training the Mouth of a Preacher's Kid: *Jeremiah 1*   129
   Kent Edwards

9. The Insanity of Stewardship: *Daniel 4*   143
   Torrey Robinson

10. Jonah's Shady Outlook from His Sunny Lookout: *Jonah 1–4*   159
    Matthew Kim

11. Can God Be Both Just and Loving? *Topical*   173
    Chris Dolson

A Word to the Reader

This is a collection of sermons based on the Old Testament. Many Christians might dismiss this effort as a waste of time. They wonder why anyone would bother with the "Old" Testament when everyone is attracted to what's "new." Walk down the aisle of a local supermarket and "new" is everywhere. From chips and dips to brooms and mops, "new" moves the merchandise. One well-known evangelical leader reports that he doesn't preach the Old Testament, only the New. He simply uses the Old Testament to illustrate New Testament teachings. Others would agree with him that the best preaching comes from passages written by Paul, Peter, James, John, Matthew, Mark, or Luke—those that are part of the "New" Testament.

Perhaps if we called the first thirty-nine books of the Bible the "First Testament" they would receive a heartier welcome. After all, the First Testament was the only Bible the first-century church possessed. As Christians gathered for teaching and worship, someone in the group would open up to a God-breathed passage from the First Testament, read it slowly, and teach what it said.

That's what the preachers who contributed to this array of sermons tried to do. Each one believes that Christians who don't regularly read or study the First Testament are losing part of our spiritual heritage.

The sermons in this collection were prepared for listeners in the twenty-first century AD. That presents challenges both for preachers and for their modern audiences. From the written conversations that follow the sermons, it's clear that each preacher wrestled not only with the message of the text but also with how that message might be heard by listeners today. How do you take passages written in the long ago and far away and help modern men and women see the eternal significance? That is a challenge whether the passage is from Leviticus or Luke.

The preachers who contributed sermons to this collection speak to all kinds of audiences. Most of the sermons were addressed to church congregations. A couple were presented to seminary audiences. One was given as an after-dinner talk. Some were preached to crowds of several thousand while others were delivered to much smaller audiences. Two were prepared and preached by women. One is a first-person narrative sermon. Keep in mind that none of the sermons were prepared with a book like this or a reader like you in mind; rather they are the product of each contributor's ordinary pulpit ministry.

All of the contributors to this volume share one thing in common: they were students of Haddon Robinson at either Denver Seminary or Gordon-Conwell Seminary. Clearly, they are not clones. They gleaned what they could use from class and put some other teaching aside. They talked about that in the conversations we had together. They are their own people.

These printed sermons resemble cadavers. Cadavers are lifeless bodies that medical students dissect to discover how muscle, sinew, and nerve are put together. While printed sermons fall far short of being living sermons with breath and fire and spirit, it is profitable to study them and see what the preachers intended to do and how they planned for the sermon to have life and coherence. In what follows, eleven preachers offer sermons on the First Testament. All but one are expository. The final sermon is a topical exposition, but we have included it to demonstrate how an evangelistic sermon can be put together.

How can this collection best be used? You could simply sit back and read each sermon, allowing God to speak to you again through his Word. However, if you want to learn how each preacher works to prepare messages every week, then read the interviews after each sermon to get a look at the creative process.

Quite a bit of content in this collection may need further explanation. If you are a student of sermons, you would be helped by reading Haddon Robinson's *Biblical Preaching*, the book that explains the theory on which these sermons are based.

God bless you as you hear these passages from the First Testament again for the first time.

1

Climbing Test Mountain

Genesis 22:1–19

BRYAN WILKERSON

S o far on this journey we've gone canoeing and caving. We've taken a road trip and walked in the woods. How about we finish with some mountain climbing? If you're a traveler, mountains represent the ultimate challenge. They are a true test of courage, skill, stamina, and commitment.

Think about how many important things happen on the tops of mountains in the Bible. Noah's ark comes to rest on top of Mount Ararat. Moses receives the Ten Commandments on Mount Sinai. Elijah defeats the prophets of Baal on Mount Carmel. The temple is built on Mount Zion. Jesus preached his most famous sermon on a mountainside, was crucified on a hill called Calvary, and ascended into heaven from the Mount of Olives.

So we shouldn't be surprised that Abraham's journey eventually leads to a mountain, and that climbing that mountain becomes the ultimate test of his faith. This morning we're going to conclude our series with one of the most compelling and disturbing stories in all of the Bible. The message is titled "Climbing Test Mountain" and our text is Genesis 22.

> Some time later God tested Abraham. He said to him, "Abraham!"
> "Here I am," he replied.
> Then God said, "Take your son, your only son, whom you love—Isaac—and go to the region of Moriah. Sacrifice him there as a burnt offering on a mountain I will show you."

Bryan Wilkerson is senior pastor of Grace Chapel in Lexington, Massachusetts. He is the author of *Living God's Story* and a frequent contributor to *Preaching Today* and *Leadership Journal*.

Early the next morning, Abraham got up and loaded his donkey. He took with him two of his servants and his son Isaac. When he had cut enough wood for the burnt offering, he set out for the place God had told him about. On the third day Abraham looked up and saw the place in the distance. He said to his servants, "Stay here with the donkey while I and the boy go over there. We will worship and then we will come back to you."

Abraham took the wood for the burnt offering and placed it on his son Isaac, and he himself carried the fire and the knife. As the two of them went on together, Isaac spoke up and said to his father Abraham, "Father?"

"Yes, my son," Abraham replied.

"The fire and wood are here," Isaac said, "but where is the lamb for the burnt offering?"

Abraham answered, "God himself will provide the lamb for the burnt offering, my son." And the two of them went on together.

When they reached the place God had told him about, Abraham built an altar there and arranged the wood on it. He bound his son Isaac and laid him on the altar, on top of the wood. Then he reached out his hand and took the knife to slay his son. But the angel of the LORD called to him from heaven, "Abraham! Abraham!"

"Here I am," he replied.

"Do not lay a hand on the boy," he said. "Do not do anything to him. Now I know that you fear God, because you have not withheld from me your son, your only son."

Abraham looked up and there in a thicket he saw a ram caught by its horns. He went over and took the ram and sacrificed it as a burnt offering instead of his son. So Abraham called that place The LORD Will Provide. And to this day it is said, "On the mountain of the LORD it will be provided."

The angel of the LORD called to Abraham from heaven a second time and said, "I swear by myself, declares the LORD, that because you have done this and have not withheld your son, your only son, I will surely bless you and make your descendants as numerous as the stars in the sky and as the sand on the seashore. Your descendants will take possession of the cities of their enemies, and through your offspring all nations on earth will be blessed, because you have obeyed me."

Then Abraham returned to his servants, and they set off together for Beersheba. (Gen. 22:1–19)

On a November evening in 1965, thirty-one-year-old Norman Morrison positioned himself on a wall outside the Pentagon in Washington, DC.

Without saying a word, he doused himself with kerosene, struck a match, and set himself ablaze. The flames shot twelve feet into the air, forming a fiery envelope around his body. Witnesses said the sound of it was like the whoosh of a small rocket fire. What made it all the more horrifying and incomprehensible was the fact that Morrison held in his arms his own baby daughter, Emily, just shy of a year old. Employees rushed out of the building and commuters jumped from their cars shouting, "Throw her down!" and "Drop the baby!" as the flames intensified.

Norman Morrison was a Quaker and a pacifist. For years he had been troubled by the war in Vietnam. More than once he'd run his hands through his hair, asking his wife, "What will it take to stop it all?" That morning Morrison read a magazine report about a Vietnamese village that had been destroyed by American bombs. The images of women and children scorched by napalm were too much for him. He borrowed a friend's old Cadillac, put Emily in the car seat and a gallon jug of kerosene in the trunk, and made the drive from Baltimore to Washington. On the way he stopped to mail a letter to his wife, which read,

Dear Anne,
    This morning, without warning, I was shown clearly what I must do. Know that I love thee, but must act for the children of the village. Then he added, "And like Abraham, I dare not go without Emily."

"Drop the baby," they cried. "Throw her down!" And at the last critical moment, he did. In his final act, the father reached out from the flames and set his daughter aside, out of harm's way. Morrison died, and that night the police placed Emily in the arms of her mother. She was unharmed and unsinged, with the aroma of kerosene still upon her.

"And like Abraham, I dare not go without Emily." I share that unsettling story because it brings to our contemporary setting all the troubling questions and emotions raised by this ancient text.

Would God really ask someone to sacrifice his own child? How could a loving parent consider such an action and come so close to doing it? Should we admire such devotion or be appalled by it?

What happened on Mount Moriah is arguably the most significant religious event in human history, apart from the life and death of Christ. Judaism, Islam, and Christianity all look to Abraham's near-sacrifice of his son as the supreme expression of devotion to God. And as the final act of Norman Morrison illustrates, the story continues to capture the imaginations of people—sometimes inspiring them to heroic or horrific acts, sometimes causing them to turn away from a God they cannot comprehend.

What are we to make of this story? What lessons does it hold for ordinary people like you and me who are making the journey of faith? Let's first experience the story as Abraham might have and then see what we can learn from it.

The Story

"Some time later," the story begins, "God tested Abraham." A better translation might be "After these things." After what things? After all that's happened to Abraham over the past twenty-five years.

After answering the call of God to a life of blessing by leaving his home in Ur and traveling hundreds of miles with his family to the land of Canaan, where he built an altar to the God who called him.

After wandering down to Egypt and taking matters into his own hands, then finding his way back to the path again.

After finding himself in a dark place where he doubted the goodness and power of God, but emerging from that darkness closer to God and stronger in his faith.

After coming to a fork in the road, where he chose to walk the less-traveled road of faith and obedience, trusting God to provide him with a son even in his old age.

After developing a relationship with God so intimate and personal that God actually visited Abraham at his tent one evening for dinner and discussed the fate of Sodom.

After finally receiving in his old age the son he'd been waiting for, Isaac, whose name means laughter.

It's been a long and winding road marked by success and failure, gains and losses. But now, at last, their future was secure, the blessing was in hand. Abraham and Sarah enjoy years of peace as they watch Isaac grow up, and they begin to enjoy the reward of trusting God.

After all that, the text says, Abraham hears that voice again. He probably hasn't heard it in a while, but it is unmistakable. "Abraham," God says. "Here I am," he answers, the response of a servant.

And then the voice asks him to do the unthinkable. "Take your son, your only son, Isaac, whom you love, and sacrifice him as a burnt offering on Mount Moriah." Now, it helps to understand that child sacrifice was common practice among the pagan peoples of Canaan. According to the fertility cults, the way to guarantee continued fruitfulness of land and livestock was for a woman to offer her firstborn as a sacrifice to the deities. It was an expression of gratitude and devotion to the gods. Remember, too, that God had not yet given the law that would forbid child sacrifice. Culturally and theologically, it would not have sounded quite as abhorrent and incongruous to Abraham as it does to us.

But on a personal level, the command to sacrifice his son was every bit as difficult for Abraham as it would be for any father. Not only did he love Isaac, as any father would, Isaac was the *child of promise*. Abraham had waited a lifetime for him. Isaac was the embodiment of everything Abraham had lived for, everything he believed about God. All his dreams for the future and the fulfillment of God's promises rested on that boy.

God knew what he was asking of Abraham. You can almost hear the sympathy in God's words, "Take your son, your only son, whom you love, and sacrifice him as a burnt offering." A burnt offering was an expression of total surrender to God. The worshiper was to take something of value—an animal or some fruit of the field—and place it on an altar where it would be totally consumed by fire, offered up entirely to God, nothing held back.

That's what God was asking Abraham to do with his greatest treasure—his only son, the child of promise.

In earlier days, Abraham would have balked at such a command, wouldn't he, based on what we've learned about him? Maybe he'd come up with another scheme or try to negotiate a different deal. Wouldn't he at least have procrastinated a bit? "God didn't say *when* I have to do this. Someday I will."

But Abraham is not the same man he was when he started out on this journey. He's grown in his faith and in relationship with God. And so early the next morning he sets out to obey the command he has been given. Notice that Abraham performed the chores himself—saddling the donkey, cutting the wood—even though he had servants. I wonder if this was his way of processing what was happening to him, of working through his grief the same way a family will preoccupy itself with hospital arrangements and medical talk when a loved one is sick.

And so they set out on their journey. The Scripture is remarkably intimate in its description of this trip. "And the two of them went on together," it says. It reminds me of a trip my father and I took when he drove me a thousand miles across the country for my freshman year at college. I was the oldest child and the first one to go away. I can recall almost every detail of that trip—the places we stopped to eat, the fleabag hotel in Toledo. As I remember, we didn't talk very much on that trip; mostly we looked out the window. But I don't think I've ever felt closer to my father than on that trip. I remember sitting in the empty dorm room after we arrived, each of us looking the other way to hide the tears that kept coming to our eyes. We both understood that something significant was happening, but we couldn't quite describe it and we certainly couldn't talk about it.

And so it must have been for Abraham and Isaac as they traveled toward the mountain of sacrifice. Not much talking but intimacy beyond words. I wonder how many times Abraham must have looked away, blinking back the tears. And Isaac was no child anymore. He certainly sensed that something significant was happening, but he didn't dare ask.

On the third day they arrived at the mountain. Abraham strapped the wood on Isaac's back and carried in his own hands the torch and the knife. "Stay here," he instructed the servants. "The boy and I will go over there and worship, and then come back to you." Did he really believe that—that both of them would return—or was he covering up, the way a soldier tells his dying comrade that he's gonna be okay?

Finally, prompted by curiosity or dread, Isaac speaks up, "Father?"

"Yes, my son." (Can you hear the tenderness?)

"Father, the wood and the fire are here, but where is the lamb for the burnt offering?" And in Abraham's answer we begin to understand what's going on in his heart.

"God himself will provide the lamb for the offering, my son." The expression translated "God will provide" literally reads, "God will see to it." After all that Abraham has been through on this journey—after working things over in his mind for these three days—Abraham has come to the place where he believes that God will come through. Somehow, some way, God will see to it that Abraham and his son will walk back down that mountain together. Perhaps God will change his mind at the last minute.

But if not, even if Abraham has to go through with it and sacrifice his son, he is convinced that God can raise his son back to life again.

The New Testament helps us here. The book of Hebrews tells us that "by faith Abraham, when God tested him, offered Isaac as a sacrifice. . . . Abraham reasoned that God could even raise the dead" (11:17–19). He reasoned. He reckoned. It's actually an accounting term meaning "to calculate." Based on all that he'd been through, Abraham had come to a place where he was willing to trust God with his greatest treasure—his only son.

When they reached the top of the mountain, Abraham himself built the altar, arranged the wood, and bound his son, laying him upon the altar. Isaac is at least twelve years old, probably older. He understands what's happening yet apparently offers no resistance. Then Abraham takes out a knife to slay his son.

What a moment that must have been. Isaac lying on the wood, looking up at his father. Abraham hesitating, looking up to heaven, as if to give God one last chance to deliver him and his son from this moment. God is testing Abraham. And Abraham, in a sense, is testing God.

And then, at the last moment, with the knife raised, that voice comes once again: "Abraham, Abraham."

How quickly do you think Abraham answered? "Here I am, Lord." A commentator points out that whenever a name is repeated in Scripture, it always indicates deep affection. "Absalom, Absalom," cries David when his son dies. "Martha, Martha," Jesus says to the woman who serves him.

"Abraham, Abraham," says God. "Don't lay a hand on the boy. Now I know that you fear God." This is *not* the fear that came over Abraham when he lied about Sarah to protect himself from Pharaoh. And it's *not* the fear that Abraham experienced in the dark night, when he doubted that God could keep his promises. This particular word indicates reverence and respect, an *affectionate* fear.

And Abraham looked up and saw a ram caught in a thicket. He unbound his son and sacrificed the ram instead, and he named the place *Jehovah Jireh*, "The Lord Will See to It." And just as he had promised, he and Isaac worshiped on that mountain and then returned to the servants. And if you think father and son were close on the way up the mountain, can you imagine the intimacy they enjoyed on the way down? The tears of joy? The confidence in God? Can you imagine when they met up with the servants who were waiting? "See, I told you we'd be back!"

And in response to Abraham's willing obedience, the Lord promises to bless Abraham with more sons and daughters than he can possibly count, and through those descendants to bless the whole world. Abraham has finally become the man God called him to be.

So that's the story. As compelling and disturbing today as it ever was. But what is the lesson? What does it mean for people like us and our journeys of faith?

The Lesson

We're told right up front that this is a *test*. But a test of what? Of love? That's how it is often interpreted and applied. That God wanted to find out whom Abraham loved more—Isaac or God. So God asked Abraham to sacrifice his son. That's a frightening thought, isn't it?

I talked to a man who was visiting a church and the pastor happened to be speaking on this story. After describing and commending Abraham's devotion, he looked out at his congregation and asked, "If God were to ask you to sacrifice your child, would you be prepared to do that?" There was silence in the room for a moment as the people swallowed hard and looked at the floor, but my friend couldn't contain himself. "No!" he shouted from his pew. It was obvious that was *not* the answer the pastor was looking for, and it made for a rather awkward moment. After the service, a teenage boy came up to the visitor and thanked him for saying no. It was the pastor's son.

Too many people have walked away from this passage fearful that God might ask them to give up their children to death. I've heard preachers say that Abraham loved Isaac too much, and that if you love someone too much God may take that person away from you. I've known people who have been afraid to get too close to God because they don't want him to ask something like this of them.

But that kind of thinking and teaching is wrongheaded; it's a misunderstanding of what this passage is all about. This was a test. That much is clear. But it was *not* a test of Abraham's *love*. It was a test of Abraham's *faith*. We know that Abraham loved God. He'd built altars to God all over Canaan. They'd had dinner together. He was God's friend. The question was not whether Abraham *loved* God. The question was whether Abraham *trusted* God. Did he believe God could still bless him, make him the father of many nations, even if he surrendered his only son into God's hands? Would he trust God with his greatest treasure—Isaac? Or would he hold back, look for another way, take matters into his own hands? That was the test—would he trust his future to God?

And that's where the story intersects with our lives. It's not asking whom you love more—God or your child, God or your spouse. You're supposed to love your child and your spouse with a fierce and loyal love. It's not a question of love, it's a question of trust. Are you prepared to trust God with your greatest treasures, with your deepest needs, with your highest hopes?

In Abraham's case, his son Isaac represented all that was dear to Abraham, so God asked him to put Isaac on the altar. But God may ask something very different of you. He might say to you, "Take your *career*—your carefully laid out career, your lifelong ambition—and offer it to me." To someone else he might say, "Take your *possessions*—your hard-earned possessions that give you a sense of security and significance—and place them in my hands." To another, "Take your *retirement* years and make them available to me." To another, "Take your *wounded heart* and place it in my tender hands." To each of us he says, "Take your *dreams . . .* take your *fears . . .* and place them on the altar." And yes, he may even say, "Take your *son* or your *daughter*, and offer them to me." Not to be killed, but to be available for his purposes, to be blessed and to be a blessing.

Understand that God is not in the business of taking children away from parents or pulling the rug out from under our dreams. But the truth is, his purposes for us are far greater than we can imagine. And if we are to fulfill those purposes we must be prepared to trust him, even with that which is nearest and dearest to us. So from time to time he will test us—asking us to *do* something, *go* somewhere, *serve* somebody in a way that feels very risky. And if we are willing to do it, he is able to bless us and others in ways we could never expect. There is no promise that we will get back everything we give up or that we will eventually get what we want. The promise is that God will see to it—he will provide what we need to live a blessed life.

The book of Hebrews tells us, "By faith Abraham offered Isaac." And what is faith? Faith is trusting ourselves to God. Abraham believed that God was going to do something on top of that mountain. He didn't know what or how or when, but he knew it would be right and good and eternally significant. And climbing that mountain was the ultimate test of that trust.

Back in high school I started rock climbing. My friend Steve introduced me to the sport. He started me out on some safe, easy climbs; top-roping, for those who are familiar with it. It was fun and challenging, and I picked it up pretty quickly. But soon it was time to try a real climb, with Steve leading and me following him up the cliff.

Steve climbed sixty or seventy feet up, then secured himself on a ledge to belay me. I worked my way up, following the route I'd seen Steve take. But then I came to an overhang, a pretty severe one that I couldn't even see around let alone climb around. I felt for a crack or a ledge or a nub to help me get up and over it, or for some other route around the overhang, but there was nothing. I hollered up to Steve, who was above the overhang, and he told me there was a solid handhold just over the lip of the overhang— what climbers call "a bucket." I could pull myself up by that. I couldn't see it, of course, so I tried to feel for it but couldn't find it.

"I can't reach it," I said.

"I know," he hollered back. "You're gonna have to go for it."

I looked down. "What do you mean go for it?"

"You gotta *commit*; you gotta let go of the rock and then reach up."

Did he say *let go* of the rock? "What if it's not there?" I said.

"Don't worry, it's there," he said.

"What if I fall?" I said.

"I'll catch you." There was a long pause, then he spoke the words I'll never forget: "Wilk, *you gotta trust me.*"

I didn't want to trust him. I wanted to trust myself. I wanted to see that handhold, or at least to feel it so I knew it was there before I reached for it. I wanted to find some other way around that overhang. But there was no other way. The only way up would be to fall away from the rock and reach. So that's what I did. And sure enough, it was there, and it was rock solid. I can feel it to this very day. And with that secure handhold I was able to push with my feet and get up and over the lip. Standing on top of that overhang was one of the best feelings I'd ever had in my life. It was just like Steve said, all I had to do was trust him.

That day on Mount Moriah, Abraham trusted God and God came through. Abraham's journey wasn't quite over yet, but when he came down from that mountain he was finally the man God had called him to be, a man through whom he would raise up a nation and a Messiah who would one day bring salvation to the whole world. Remember, the journey isn't just about getting there; it's about who you become along the way. Abraham had become the friend of God and the father of faith.

Some of us are climbing Test Mountain right now. God is probing, proving your faith. He wants to meet you on that mountain, to do something good and eternally significant. Others of us will find ourselves on that mountain in the year or years to come. Are we prepared to trust him with that which is nearest and dearest to us—our careers, our relationships, our health, our finances, our ministries? And most important, are we prepared to trust him with our very souls?

A Greater Sacrifice

By now you have probably recognized that there is something bigger going on here than the near-sacrifice of Isaac. Something is being foreshadowed—something that Abraham anticipated by faith, though he could not possibly have understood it fully.

Thousands of years later, on a hill very near to this one, a greater Father offered a greater Son as a sacrifice. Not as a burnt offering but as a sin offering, as payment for the crimes of humanity. Only this time when an arm was raised to deal a deadly blow, there was no voice from heaven to stay the hand. This time when the Father looked around, there was no substitute to take the Son's place. The Son himself was the substitute—for you and for me and for everyone. On that day, young Isaac's question was finally answered: "Father, where is the Lamb for the offering?" Jesus Christ, by his sacrificial death on the cross, became the Lamb of God, taking away the sins of the world. "On the mountain of the Lord it will be provided," Abraham predicted. And so it was.

So maybe it's a love story after all. Not about Abraham's love for God, but about God's love for Abraham, meeting him in such a powerful way. And God's love for us, offering us forgiveness of sin and eternal life.

The journey of a lifetime begins and ends right here—at the cross of Christ where we meet the God we can trust. We can trust him with our greatest treasures; we can trust him with our deepest needs; we can trust him with our highest hopes. We can trust him with our very souls. For if God did not spare his own Son, but gave him up for us all, how will he not also, along with Jesus, give us everything we need to be blessed, and to be a blessing to others?

Commentary

Good preaching is always somewhat emotional. It appeals to the mind and to the feelings of the listeners. This passage in Genesis 22 is one of the most emotional in that book as well as in the entire Bible. The difficulty, however, is that we may read the passage and draw from it the wrong emotion. The text is not telling Abraham to sacrifice Isaac as the pagans would sacrifice their children to get the favor of a god. The offering here has to do with God's promise. God has said it would be through Isaac that the world will be blessed. If Isaac is killed, then God's promise is rendered worthless. This is a sermon about God and faith.

In Bryan Wilkerson's sermon, the focus on the emotions is in the right place. One danger of this focus on emotion is that we may illustrate it with story material that touches our listeners. Actually, the real task is to take the passage and see where the biblical writer wants to focus the emotions and then try to do that in the sermon. Years ago, old-time preachers knew how to use the conclusion to drive home the point through the use of the story. The story was something emotional but not necessarily something that came out of the Bible. I think Bryan has done a splendid job in discussing the text, and I think the questions and answers he gives provide understanding for issues preachers are faced with in the world today.

Interview

How do you go about preparing to preach?

It starts with advance work. A few times a year, just about every season, I go away for a couple of days to lay out the next three months, the next season of preaching. For those few days, it's nonstop Bible commentaries and yellow legal pad. I try to chart everything out. I get a text and a big idea for every week of the series. Once I've got that, then there's the weekly prep; for me that's almost always about twenty hours, sometimes a little less. I prepare the week I preach, so I really don't work too far ahead other than those retreat weekends. Each week I write the sermon I'm preaching that Sunday, much to the chagrin of all the creative people on my team who wish I were two or three weeks ahead. But I've never been able to do that.

I preach so much out of my own experience and what's happening in the life of the church and the culture that week. There's an immediacy about it that I really like and that I think helps the preaching. The downside is that it's hard on the creative team to keep up and be prepared, so we try to strike a balance. On Monday morning I get out my yellow legal pad. I still use a legal pad for my creative work. The first page is free association. I start writing down ideas, things that are on my mind, potential illustrations, title possibilities. It's a creative page that I keep handy and mark up all week long.

Then I start doing my exegetical work—usually on Monday morning for a couple of hours and Tuesday morning for a few hours—trying to work for an outline, big idea, that sort of thing. I leave it alone on Wednesday because I have meetings all day. Thursday is a big writing day. I get up early and work until about one o'clock to sketch an outline and start typing a manuscript, and I try to get half or two-thirds of the way done. I do a little more on Friday morning. Hopefully by Friday I'm pretty much done with my draft and Saturday I'm tuning it up—adding in any visuals, bullet points, pictures, anything we might want to insert in the message. I probably spend another five or six hours on Saturday.

That's a full schedule. Do you take time off?

Typically Fridays, but I cheat a little bit. I work before breakfast for a couple of hours. It's my best time of day. I work on Saturday catch-as-catch-can. I get up early and try to spend the day either with the family or just relax or work around the house, but then I sneak in a couple of hours here and there and then usually again at night just to keep it fresh in my mind. Then I'll get up super early on Sunday morning and spend two or three more hours. Hopefully at that point I'm just learning it, practicing it.

What about commentaries? Do you use them? When do you go to them?

Pretty early. Part of my retreat work involves skimming through the commentaries. But then I really like to do it all again the week I'm preaching. I'll probably spend an additional three hours in commentaries the week I preach.

What about illustrations? Where do you find them? Do you collect them?

They come from my daily and weekly reading. I get a lot of illustrations out of the *New York Times*. I'll walk through a museum on my day off. From time to time I save things and stick them in the file somewhere. I still use Haddon's system of numbered file folders. My administrator keeps a list of them. The internet helps a lot because you can Google things and find recent articles. I find that most of that stuff triggers my imagination to remember my own experience. I may not use the story I read about, but

I think, "Oh yeah, something like that happened to me once," and I can make it more personal.

What role does your audience play in determining preaching passages and series?

We have three thousand or so adults on a Sunday. I do a lot of my sermon planning collaboratively with the pastoral team. We have a theme for the year, and we craft what's called the "teaching journey" from September to June. We try to cover different kinds of biblical material and different kinds of topical issues that we can loosely organize around that particular theme. We'll sit together as a staff and ask, "What are we hearing from the congregation? Are we in a building program? Are we growing? Are we shrinking? Are we in conflict?"

Who is involved in that planning?

The whole ministry staff. I like to include everyone so they all feel like they have a stake in helping to shape the teaching journey.

Let's talk about this sermon from Genesis 22. What are the challenges in preaching a well-known but very misunderstood text?

I think the challenge is to help the listeners get past either the bad teaching they've received on that passage or the misunderstandings they have. Passages like this one are emotionally loaded, and attempts have been made to explain or apply it in what I think are poor ways. You have to help people get past their fear and their misunderstandings without sounding like a know-it-all. (In other words, "Everything you read on this was wrong and now I'm going to straighten you out.") You have to make the journey first. You have to deal with everything you've heard about that passage and confront your own fears and misunderstandings. You have to ask, "What does this text actually say, and can I approach it with a blank slate?"

What's the best way to avoid being stale as a preacher?

Do your own work, don't just default to what you've heard other people say. Don't read five other preachers' sermons on a passage. Get out the commentaries and sit with the text for a long time. Read another passage and turn it over in your head. Go for a run, take a walk, write in a journal. Ask the Lord to bring you your own insights, and then you have something fresh to offer.

How do you tell the story with insight and get listeners emotionally involved?

A big part is using your imagination. You really have to imagine what it must have been like to play out that scenario. Sit for a little while and imagine how Abraham felt. If you're a father, think about your own son, about taking a walk with him and how that would feel. Then imagine it from Isaac's perspective and from the servants' perspective. That's when doing your own homework and sitting with the text makes all the difference. Ask, "What does it feel like?" The problem with the Old Testament is that those stories, as Haddon says, are long ago and far away.

How do you deal with applying the "long ago and far away" to a modern audience?

I try to ask, "What's a similar situation in today's world?" That's when I came up with the idea of taking your firstborn child off to college. It's a rite of passage that's full of emotion and uncertainty. That enabled me to get inside both Abraham's and Isaac's emotions. Interestingly, when I first preached that sermon years and years ago, I told the story more from remembering my father dropping me off at college. Now I've dropped off four kids of my own at college. It feels a little different from the father's point of view.

After the Scripture is read, you begin with a disturbing story. Why start out that way?

I think you have to name the difficulty and say it up front and give people permission to say, "I don't get this story" or "I don't like this story." It's okay to feel that way about the Bible. I started with that really disturbing story about the guy and his daughter because that helps us feel it, and our intuitive reaction is just terrible. When you give people permission to be bothered by this story, then they can listen with fresh ears.

I knew a woman who said this story ruined God for her.

So say that up front and then that woman thinks, "Oh, okay. This preacher knows me and knows what I'm thinking, and it's okay for me to feel this way about this story." She doesn't have to have her defenses up.

Do you use notes when you preach?

I use notes, way more than I should.

I've seen you preach and I never knew you used them. How do you use notes and still sound conversational?

I'm pretty good at not being dependent on notes, but I always have them. So what I do now is I bring my printed manuscript to the pulpit with me, but I don't print it on full-size paper. The manuscript is the same size as my Bible pages, so it almost looks like I have only my Bible with me. I'm not shuffling letter-size pages, and it looks like I'm working from a Bible. I try to know the content well enough that I just peek once in a while to know what comes next.

Any advice to someone who preaches with a manuscript?

The thing about manuscripts is saying it and not reading it. A lot of preachers think that if they just read over the manuscript twenty times, they'll deliver the sermon fluently, but all they do is read it fluently. You have to stop reading it in your preparation and just say it. Have it in front of you and take a peek, but do it conversationally. One of my weekly drills involves driving over to church on Sunday morning. It's a twelve-minute drive, so I can say my introduction and conclusion to myself. When you say it to yourself out loud, it makes all the difference in the world.

Honestly, my biggest frustration with my preaching is that I'm too dependent on my notes. The computer has ruined me, because back in the day I handwrote it all. I was a lousy typist, so I didn't type my sermons. I kept making handwritten notes, and the mechanics of doing that just got it in my head. And the other thing about the computer is that it makes you such a wordsmith that you fall in love with your sentences and you can't let it go. You have to be word perfect. You have to read it because you're afraid you'll mess it up.

I suppose that's the disadvantage of preaching without notes?

You miss stuff. You do.

What about technology? How do you incorporate that?

We put the text on the screen. Usually I'll put the big idea and what we call "the story line" up on the screen so people can write that down verbatim if they want to. If there's a lot of instructional stuff I may put up some bullet points, but I don't like to. If I feel like there's a lot of ground that we've got to cover here and this will help people stay with me, then I'll use them. And the listeners like to take notes.

Is there a downside to using visuals?

I always tell preachers, every time you put something on the screen people stop paying attention to you. You lose eye contact and you have to win it back again. It's probably true that what's on the screen is more interesting than you. Don't set yourself up for that kind of competition.

Tell me about the sermon in terms of the overall flow of the worship service.

The sermon isn't the message. The service is the message. We talk about the journey of the service: what journey are we taking people on today? The sermon is obviously a big part of it, but it's only a part. We try to connect as much as we can in terms of content, Scripture reading, and lyrics to songs. Is this a message about comforting people? If it is, then our music should be comforting. If this is a message about inspiring people to go out and conquer the world, then the music had better be inspirational.

How does working with a large staff affect your preaching preparation?

I spend a lot of time with the creative team. We do a two-hour worship planning meeting every week, and every other week we do a two-hour creative meeting where we're not actually planning a particular service, we're just looking ahead and saying, "All right, we're going to be talking about trials in the next series. What are some songs, video clips, illustrations, dramas?" We do those creative meetings twice a month and then the weekly planning meeting.

Your staff must really feel like they're part of things.

Yes, they really do. Again, the frustration is that I'm not always far enough ahead. Usually three weeks ahead I have my idea, my text, and a couple of key thoughts. They usually have enough to go on three weeks in advance, but it's not like sitting down with a written sermon a week or two in advance.

What advice would you give to a young preacher?

Do your own homework. It's too easy these days to access and download and scavenge other people's work. It's okay to do that a little bit, but do your own homework first and maybe augment if you know somebody has good illustrations or something like that. Once you get someone else's outline in your head, it's almost impossible to come up with your own outline.

What encouragement would you give to a more seasoned preacher?

Articulate what your own style is. In the early years of your preaching, you're learning from other preachers. You're following your mentors from seminary, but you're still finding your own voice. What do you do well? What makes your preaching effective in terms of structure, content, theme, and delivery? What's your sweet spot? Know who you are and get comfortable with who you are and lean into it. After ten years, now you have your own voice. You're good at things. Preachers can learn to articulate: "What am I good at? What's my style?" You can lean into that and feel confident.

2

How to Say God's Name

Exodus 20:7

Eric Dokken

Some of you have seen *Antiques Roadshow*, a program on PBS where the show's producers rent out a convention hall and have people bring in stuff that they have in their attics or basements. They've either had this stuff in their family for a number of years or they just found it at the dump a few weeks before, but they bring in all this junk to find out if it actually has any value. As it turns out, most of it is really junk . . . but some of it actually does have some value.

For example, one guy who apparently goes to the dump looking for treasure came in with a book of paintings. The appraiser was looking at it and said, "Do you know anything about it?"

"Well, I think it's Asian," responded the man.

The appraiser looked through the book. It contained a number of paintings of wildlife. After talking about it for a little bit, he said, "You could probably get about $6,000 for it." Not a bad day at the dump.

Another lady brought in a red vase that she had gotten from her mother's family about thirty years earlier. It had been sitting in a cabinet so that the kids couldn't play with it. She had no idea how much it was worth. The appraiser looked at it and said, "Well, this actually happens to be Tiffany glass, and a special kind of Tiffany glass." He told her that if she brought it to a retail store she could get $25,000 for it.

Eric Dokken is pastor of Grace Community Church in Marblehead, Massachusetts. He also serves as a sermon evaluator at Gordon-Conwell Theological Seminary.

Another guy came in with a painting—kind of cool looking—but just a painting of a girl with a fancy dress. It looked kind of old and it had a signature up on the corner. The appraiser asked, "How did you get it?"

The man explained, "Well, I used to be in this band called Gypsy, and we wanted some inspiration for an album cover. I saw this picture, fell in love with it, paid $200 for it."

"Well, if you look at this signature here . . . it happens to be by someone quite famous—an Italian artist who now just happens to be incredibly popular. If you were to get this painting cleaned up, you could sell this painting for $75,000."

The guy was completely shocked! And as I'm watching this program, I'm wondering what I can dig out of my room that would be worth $75,000. That's what happens as you watch a program like that, you begin to wonder, "Do I have some kind of treasure in my house that I could get some money for?" Maybe some of you do, but most of us don't. Most of us will continue to get by but not be extremely wealthy.

But this morning I want to talk to you about a different treasure, a treasure that each one of us has. Like the people on *Antiques Roadshow*, maybe we don't know we have it. It's a treasure that's much more valuable than some paintings or a vase. It's a treasure that we can find in the Scripture that was read earlier. If you'd like to look in your Bibles with me, turn to Exodus 20; we're going to ask, "What is this treasure?"

Many of you recognize this as the Ten Commandments. This is the first time they appear in the Bible. They also appear in Deuteronomy 5. And in the Ten Commandments, the Lord establishes the principles by which his people are to live in covenant with him, the Lord who rescued them from slavery. And in Exodus 20:7 we find the third commandment, "You shall not misuse the name of the LORD your God, for the LORD will not hold anyone guiltless who misuses his name." You'll see in the third commandment that God is very concerned about his name. In the Old Testament, people in general were very concerned about their names.

Names were a very big deal. God named the first man Adam, which simply means "man." Then Adam named Eve because she'd be the mother of all the living. And through the entire Old Testament parents are giving children names that are significant. Sarah names her son Isaac because she laughed when she found out she would be pregnant. Hannah prayed for years for a son, and when she finally gets a son she names him Samuel, which means "heard of God" because God heard her prayer. Throughout the Old Testament, parents give their children names that are significant. They make a big deal out of names, and God cares so much about names that sometimes he even changes people's names. Abram becomes Abraham. Sarai becomes Sarah. Simon becomes Peter.

Names are a big deal, and God is saying in the third commandment, "My name is a big deal. My name is a treasure." God's name is the treasure that each one of us has. That doesn't seem like all that great of a treasure, does it?

In our culture, names aren't nearly as important as they were back in the Old Testament. For instance, the most popular name for females in the United States last year was Emma. Emma means something like "universal." Either you have really high ideals for your daughter or you just didn't think about what that name meant when you named her. The third most popular name for girls is Madison. I think Madison is a beautiful name, but if you look up the meaning of Madison it's "son of a mighty warrior." It would be really hard for your daughter to live up to that name.

If you go on Facebook, there is a page that is called "If this page gets 500,000 likes I will name my son Batman." It's posted by a guy living in the UK, and he says if 500,000 people think it's a good idea, he will name his son Batman. That's because names don't mean as much as they did in Old Testament culture.

But they do mean something, don't they? If you go to the Batman page on Facebook and read the comments, you'll see most of the comments say something like, "This is the worst idea I've ever heard of" or "Who is this child's mother and how could she let the father do this?"

We care about names. I care about my name. People often spell my name with a *k*—E-R-I-K. It bugs me when people mess up my name.

And you like people to get your name right too, don't you? We care about our names. That's why in Exodus 20:7, the third commandment, God says, "Don't misuse my name. My name is important. My name is a treasure."

What is so significant about God's name, especially in the book of Exodus, is that it's a way for God to identify himself in relationship with his people. As some of you may notice, the name LORD is in small capital letters. That's because it doesn't actually say "Lord" there. It really says God's name, which is Yahweh—the name by which God revealed himself to the people of Israel. Yahweh. The people took this command so seriously in the Old Testament that they didn't want to pronounce the name Yahweh, so it eventually got translated as LORD (with small caps) and we have continued that tradition today.

So you can say you've learned something today. Maybe you didn't know this before. Every time you see LORD with small caps it really means Yahweh. Yahweh, the name God revealed to establish a relationship with his people. That's what knowing someone's name does.

When I was in junior high, I went to camp. I went to camp, of course, to learn about God . . . but I had another motive . . . to meet girls. I'm not endorsing this as a reason for going to camp, but the last time I was there we went around and everyone said his or her name. I had been watching, and there was one girl whom I wanted to get to know. I paid very close attention when she said her name so that later I could come up and say, "Hey, Stephanie, I'm Eric," because a name establishes a relationship.

If you don't know someone's name, it's really hard to make any progress in a relationship. So God reveals his name to his people as Yahweh because he establishes a relationship with them. That is the name by which the Israelites know him and it is a treasure.

God's name is a treasure to us as well, not simply because it establishes a relationship but because it says something about his character. It's the same in our culture as well. When I say someone's name you don't just hear a name, you think about a person. If I say Mother Teresa, you would think about an angelic person. If I say Adolf Hitler, you would think of someone very different.

A lot of you know the name Bernie Madoff. He's a guy who swindled his friends and a lot of other people out of lots and lots of money. At Gordon-Conwell last year, there was a student whose name was very close to Madoff. I accidentally called him Madoff, and he was very quick to say, "No, it's Modaf." He didn't want his name associated with this guy named Bernie Madoff.

A person's name represents not only a sound but also the person's character. In Exodus 33, Moses is begging God to do something, to give him a sign to show that he is really with Moses and with the Israelite people. So God says, "Here is what I'll do: I'll make my goodness pass before you and I will proclaim my name." Then in Exodus 34 he takes Moses and sets him in a little place behind some rocks that he can look over. And then the Lord passes over Moses, and Moses sees the Lord, and then the text says the Lord proclaims, "The LORD, the LORD," which is of course, "Yahweh, Yahweh, the compassionate and gracious God, slow to anger, abounding in love and faithfulness" (Exod. 34:6). That's God's character, "The LORD, the LORD, slow to anger, gracious and compassionate." God's character is bound up in his name, and that's why God wants us to take his name seriously—to handle his name with care.

You'll notice in the NIV that it says, "Do not misuse the name of the LORD your God," but most of you here this morning know that the older translations say, "Do not use the name of the LORD your God in vain." The literal translation is something like, "Do not lift up the name of the LORD your God to something that is vain or worthless. Do not use it for something that has no value"—because God's name is a treasure that shouldn't be used in those contexts.

The primary application of this commandment in the Old Testament was perjury—to make an oath based on the name of the Lord that you did not intend to keep. You would say, "By God's name I swear I will do this or that," when in your heart you had no intention of keeping that promise. If you do that you are taking the name of the Lord your God in vain. You are misusing the name of the Lord. You are saying in a sense, "God doesn't exist," because you swear by the name of the Lord and then you don't do what you promised. You are saying, "God doesn't exist," and you are making him very, very small. You're using the name of the Lord your God in vain.

We can misuse God's name in other ways as well. You usually hear the name of the Lord in our culture when people are really angry or people are really surprised. Suddenly you hear the name of the Lord come out of their mouths in these contexts, and it has nothing to do with who our great and awesome God is. They are not thinking about the actual Jesus Christ who died for our sins and is now seated at the right hand of God. They are taking God's character and who he is lightly.

And also we say the name of the Lord in different ways, so somehow we are moving around the commandment or finding a loophole. We'll say "gosh" or "geez" instead of God or Jesus. We're still referring to God's name, aren't we? We're still using the name of the Lord in vain. God says don't use my name in situations that make me look small . . . in situations that don't reflect who I am, the God who makes a covenant with his people. Don't misuse the name of the Lord your God.

And he takes his name so seriously that he says, "Whoever misuses my name I will not leave unpunished" or "I will not hold anyone guiltless who misuses my name." How does God intend to punish people who misuse his name? I can give you a few examples from the Bible.

In Leviticus 24 there's a young man who curses the name of the Lord. He takes the name of the Lord in vain. The Israelites go to Moses and ask, "What should we do?" Moses says, "We're going to have everyone who heard him come together and we are going to have to kill this man by stoning." That is a very extreme punishment for misusing the name of the Lord.

In the New Testament it's a little bit different. There are some guys called the seven sons of Sceva. Their father's name is Sceva—he's a Jewish priest. They realize the name of Jesus is powerful. They hear Paul use it. And so they decide they are going to cast out a demon in the name of Jesus because they have seen what it can do. They see a guy who is possessed by a demon and they say, "In the name of Jesus, we cast you out." The guy looks at them and says, "I know who Jesus is, and I've heard of Paul who preaches in the name of Jesus, but I don't know who you are." And then the guy jumps on them, starts beating them, tears off their robes, and kicks them out of the house. They were punished for taking the name of the Lord in vain.

Now that probably won't happen to us. I've never seen it happen when I've heard someone misuse the name of the Lord. But I do think this command is serious—"I will not leave them unpunished, those who misuse the name of the Lord." It's a divine way of saying, "I wouldn't do that if I were you." God is saying, "If you don't treasure my name, if you don't use my name in a way that reflects my character, then I will not leave you unpunished."

One punishment is simply that we forget how valuable God is. We forget that God is our treasure when we consistently misuse the name of the Lord.

So the way to use God's name appropriately, the way to handle God's name with care, is to make sure that every time we say the name of the Lord, every time the name of the Lord crosses our lips, we are treasuring the Lord in our hearts. We do that by thinking about the character and person of God and who he is and what he has revealed to us. We do that by using his name in a way that is consistent with his character. When we treasure the name of God, we will treasure God himself. We will treasure God by treasuring God's name.

I've been reading a book on youth ministry, and the author tells a story about being invited to a church to talk about youth ministry. He attended a worship service and sat toward the front. He looked over to the side and saw a bunch of youth sitting across from him. They were pretty restless, making a lot of noise and talking to each other and just sort of drawing attention to themselves. As the service began, they continued to talk and disrupt the service. Finally, toward the end of the service, the congregation celebrated communion. One of the ladies who was serving communion was an older lady, probably in her late seventies. She stood there as each person came up. In their tradition they would say, "The body of Christ broken for you," and she did this as each person came up.

Then the youth went to the back and started to come forward, and the author noticed that something happened to the woman. She started to get very emotional and she actually started to weep. She continued to serve communion, and as the youth were walking forward they continued to be disruptive. The people in the pews were saying, "Shhh! Shhh! Quiet!" but they weren't listening. And the author was watching to see what would happen when they got to the front.

This lady was bawling her eyes out and they weren't even paying attention, and he was wondering if he'd have to get out of his seat and help her. But as the first youth approached her and she was holding the communion plate, crying, she said, "The body of Christ broken for you, Thomas. . . . The body of Christ broken for you, Sarah." And as each youth came through she said the same thing—calling each one of them by name.

He asked her afterward what had happened: "You seemed quite emotional during worship today." And she said, "Well, I was asked a few years ago to serve the youth group, but I'm too old to do anything with them so I said I would pray. So someone took their picture and wrote prayer requests on the back and wrote their names." She had been praying for them by name for years, but this was the first opportunity for her to serve communion to them. As they came she suddenly realized she knew their names, and she was serving them communion in the name of the Lord Jesus Christ.

I cannot think of any better way to use the name of the Lord than by saying, "The body of Christ broken for you." When we use the name of the Lord, we should say it in a way that we are treasuring him in our hearts and thinking of his character. As his name crosses our lips, we are treasuring the name of the Lord. When we treasure the name of the Lord, we treasure God himself.

The name of the Lord is quite a powerful and valuable thing. When the Lord reveals his name to Moses, he tells him, "I am going to send you to release the Israelites." And Moses asks, "Who should I say sent me?" God says, "Tell them that Yahweh sent you," which means "I Am Who I Am." The name Yahweh means the One who exists without the help of anyone else. I Am Who I Am. The all-powerful One who will do what he wants to do.

Commentators have pointed out that everyone has received a name from someone. Most of us were named by our parents. God is the only one who wasn't named by someone else. God named himself. He gave himself the name Yahweh, which means "I Am Who I Am," the all-powerful One. That's one of God's names.

Another one of God's names was given to a baby who was born to a poor girl in a village called Bethlehem. And though the prophet said he would be called "Wonderful Counselor, Everlasting Father, Prince of Peace, Almighty God"—though the prophet said that, he grew up simply as Jesus of Nazareth, the carpenter's son. He was a man who didn't have a name. Then he was crucified with nameless criminals. But the apostle Paul tells us the Lord raised him from the dead. The Lord gave him "the name that is above every name, that at the name of Jesus every knee should bow, in heaven and on earth and under the earth, and every tongue confess that Jesus Christ is Lord" (Phil. 2:9–10). That's a powerful name. That's a treasure that each one of us has been given. You treasure God by treasuring his name.

I could point to places all over the Bible where it says this, but the most well known, and the one you will recognize, comes from the Lord's Prayer. "Our Father, who art in heaven, *hallowed be thy name*." God knows that if you get his name right, if you treasure his name, you will ultimately treasure him.

Watching *Antiques Roadshow* it's interesting to see these people hauling all their stuff on wagons and carts. And after they talk to the appraiser and suddenly find out how much their stuff is worth, their attitude toward it changes. When the lady found out her vase was worth $25,000 she said, "I should probably get some insurance on that." When the guy found out his painting was worth $75,000 he said, "I should probably get that cleaned." Their attitude changed when they realized how much the item was worth.

This morning I've been talking to you about God's name. God's name is a treasure that he has given to each one of us. God's name establishes a relationship with us. God's name is powerful, and it would be best if we didn't treat his name lightly, if we didn't misuse the name of the Lord our God. Instead we should treasure the name of the Lord our God. In treasuring God's name, we treasure God himself.

Commentary

The sermons in this collection all start out well. Strong introductions get attention, bring a need to the surface, and orient listeners to the body of the message. All of these preachers do that—and do it well. Eric Dokken begins by referring to a popular television program. That gets and holds attention.

The need of the sermon comes right after the introduction. Dokken raises the question, "Do I have some kind of treasure in my house that I can get some money for?" Then he goes on to say, "Like the people on *Antiques Roadshow*, maybe we don't know we have it. It's a treasure that's much more valuable than some paintings or a vase."

This is about one of the Ten Commandments that deals with God's name. As you read through the sermon, notice how Dokken takes time to expand on the importance of names. He does it positively and negatively. Then he introduces God's name—Yahweh. In fact, in the development of his sermon Dokken uses illustrations that are specific and down to earth. A potential problem with a sermon like this is that it can have no application to people in the twenty-first century, but Dokken shows, with examples and admonition, the danger of not getting God's name right.

Interview

How do you prepare to preach?

I try to spend time in the text doing my own work before looking at anyone else's. I begin by translating the passage. The more time I can spend looking at the language, at the text itself without looking at commentaries, the more I find that time valuable.

When do you look for the central idea?

That comes once I feel I have a good understanding of the passage and I look at the commentaries. I'm often surprised at what I've missed when I read the commentaries. I find some pretty interesting insights there. I average about five or six hours in exegesis, including time in the commentaries. Then I begin to figure out the central idea. It's a pretty painful, long process.

How many hours do you spend preparing a sermon?

About fifteen to twenty hours.

What's the most challenging part of the sermon preparation process?

Determining the exegetical subject and complement. I find that to be the hardest stage. Next is coming up with the homiletical idea of the sermon.

I find that requires the most intense thinking. If I don't feel confident in that stage, I won't feel confident in the sermon.

Once I have that, I construct and fill in the outline. During that time I've been writing down ideas for support material, my introduction, and my conclusion.

When do you determine sermon structure?

Once I have the homiletical idea. The idea shapes the form for the sermon.

Your central idea was repeated many times. Is that typical?

Yes. I try to repeat my central idea in different parts of the sermon. The first time I say it, I take great care in restating it and repeating it.

This sermon is inductive-deductive?

I didn't land on the central idea until about the middle of the sermon. It sort of developed inductively: "God's name is a treasure." I explained why it was a treasure, and toward the middle of the sermon I said, "We treasure God by treasuring his name" and "When we treasure the name of God, we will treasure God himself." The idea builds and then it's stated in the middle of the sermon.

Inductive sermons are really hard. I think you have to be a very good communicator to preach effective inductive sermons.

Did you face any difficulties in preaching an expository sermon on one verse?

It was challenging because I really wanted to put it in context but didn't feel that I had the time to do that.

Was this part of a sermon series?

No, I preached it as a stand-alone message.

What was the challenge in applying this message?

Bridging the gap between the two cultures. There's an obvious emphasis on names in Hebrew culture and less so in ours. I tried to bring that out and then convey to the audience the idea that you do care about your name.

Did your illustrations help you to do that?

Yes. I showed that we do care about names when I said how I feel when people use my own name and how people responded to Batman. Once I felt that I had convinced them names are important in our culture, it seemed a little more obvious how important it was that we use God's name correctly. It has to do with our relationship with God and how we feel about him. In our culture we don't tend to say things like, "I swear on the Bible" or "I swear by God" anymore. It seems like our primary violation is that we use God's name casually, and so that followed the value of the name. If we recognize the name is a treasure, then we will guard the way we use it.

I think it's interesting that we find loopholes. We say God's name in different ways. It's actually a sensitive topic for people. There was some pushback on that specific idea because it's such a part of the way we talk and we hear it so regularly.

A good application of your idea was found in communion. You said, "I cannot think of any better way to use the name of the Lord than by saying, 'The body of Christ broken for you.'" Tell me about linking your message to communion.

I think that communion should be an integral part of the service rather than something that's tacked on. But I don't find it difficult to do that, because it seems to me that the central theme of the Bible leads toward Christ's crucifixion, burial, and resurrection. Every verse and passage in the Bible will have a fairly obvious connection to that. As I preach the gospel and the message, those roads to communion are often easy to find.

Tell me about your illustrations. They're vivid. Where do you find them?

I save them in a folder on my computer. It's more about looking for them in the world around you than it is about finding them in your file system. So despite the thousands I have in my computer, in most sermons I use illustrations that are fresh. They're not from that file. It's about looking for them.

My favorite resources are Christian literature and listening to other preachers and the illustrations that they use. In the end, the majority of my sermon illustrations are from life experiences that I personally have had or have observed in other people. I think in using those you find a lot more overlap with your audience.

Because of that, I felt less comfortable with my final illustration about the lady serving communion. I thought it fit well, it accomplished what I wanted to accomplish there, but I was one step removed from it. It didn't have as much impact as it might have if it was something I personally experienced.

Anything you'd do differently in this sermon?

One struggle was the length. I think that it is possible to have a good sermon that is shorter, more concise.

I struggled with the homiletical idea. The command itself is stated in the negative. My idea was stated in the positive because I think that even though the Ten Commandments are stated negatively, they do more than prohibit. They actually reflect a positive principle. When I preached it again, I changed the idea to something I had used in the sermon that was sort of the idea behind it: "When you take God's name on your lips, treasure his character in your heart," which was a more practical way of fleshing out the idea. And I think that reflected the more practical nature of the commandment rather than the general principle behind it. If I had to change something, I'd make the idea a little more practical.

How long have you been preaching?

About twelve years.

What advice would you give to a young preacher?

It's important to master the basics. Be able to communicate an idea clearly and not worry as much about being extremely eloquent or profound. As you grow in your ability and comfort in the pulpit, you can begin to apply some more creativity to your preaching. Work hard on the basics of preaching.

You don't write a manuscript. Why not?

Because of my learning style, it's much easier for me to verbally, audibly talk through a sermon than to type it out.

So you talk through it. What does that look like?

If I sit in front of the computer, I have a difficult time typing because I type so much slower than I talk or think. I have the outline and talk through it, and I'm able to visualize how the pieces fit together and edit it that way.

But you write a detailed outline?

Yes.

Do you preach without notes?

I do.

Why?

It forces me to internalize the message, and then I'm able to adjust to the audience. I'm not looking down at a piece of paper. I spend so much time thinking about the idea and the outline that it's automatically internalized.

The increased eye contact is valuable. People don't respond to outlines as much as they do to a person. I can look directly at them.

What would you want your congregation to say about your preaching?

I would want them to say that they love God and they love their neighbor after listening to Eric's sermons.

3

The Story of the Left-Handed Assassin and the Obese King

Judges 3:12–30

S TEVE M ATHEWSON

Today I am going to preach from one of the most neglected books of the Bible. It's a book that few pastors dare to preach—maybe a story or two, but for the most part we avoid it. When I told the ministry staff at our church a couple years ago that I was going to preach through this book, they gave me a look that said, "You've got to be kidding." The book to which I am referring is the book of Judges. We pastors tend to avoid it. It seems an unlikely book to stimulate our growth as Christ-followers, and there are two big reasons why.

First, Judges is story. Stories are for little kids, aren't they? We look at Bible stories as juvenile. Children study Bible stories—brought to life with flannelgraph figures or VeggieTales videos—in the basement of the church building while the big people upstairs study the apostle Paul's letters. But despite our prejudice, narrative is actually one of the most sophisticated ways—if not *the* most sophisticated way—of communicating truth. According to the apostle Paul in 2 Timothy 3:16–17, "All Scripture"—and that includes Old Testament stories—"is God-breathed and is useful for teaching, rebuking, correcting and training in righteousness, so that the servant of God may be thoroughly equipped for every good work."

Steve Mathewson is senior pastor of CrossLife Evangelical Free Church in Libertyville, Illinois. He also teaches preaching as an adjunct professor at Trinity Evangelical Divinity School and Moody Bible Institute, and as a professor in the Doctor of Ministry program at Denver Seminary. He is the author of five books, including three on preaching: *The Art of Preaching Old Testament Narrative*, *Preaching the Four Gospels with Confidence*, and *Preaching the Hard Words of Jesus*. He previously served as a pastor in Montana for twenty years and taught preaching at Montana Bible College.

But there's a second reason why we neglect this book. Judges is a dark, bizarre book! If you made a movie out of Judges, it would be rated R for violence and sex. By the end of the book, you've got a guy whose concubine gets gang-raped, and then he responds by cutting her into twelve pieces and FedExing them to all the areas of Israel. What in the world is that doing in the Bible?

Yes, the story line of Judges is dark and depressing. Basically, the message of the book is that God's people self-destruct when they live like their pagan neighbors. But God is at work. And if you read the story with care, you will learn what God is like and how he operates in all ages—even in the darkest times.

Today I want to share a story from Judges that, quite honestly, I am almost embarrassed to preach. It's a crude, off-color story; a story with a bit of bathroom humor; a story that pokes fun at one man's obesity. That's not my kind of story. Yet it is my kind of story because it's about God and how he gets his people through hopeless situations. How can we carry out the mission God has given to us when we run up against hopeless situations? How can we ever hope to overcome the consequences of our own sin or someone else's sin so that we can do something significant for God? Please turn to Judges 3:12–30.

The story begins in verse 12 with a familiar refrain: "Again the Israelites did evil in the eyes of the LORD." This started a vicious chain of events—familiar to you if you know anything about the book of Judges. Israel rebelled. God sent an enemy people to get their attention. The Israelites cried out to God. God raised up a deliverer to rescue the people from the enemy. Together, the individual stories form a main story line. The main story line of Judges is about Israel getting caught in a vicious cycle of rebellion, which left the nation in worse shape at the end of the story than at the beginning. The book of Judges as a whole tells us that God's people needed something more. Their slide into evil was so devastating that they could never get completely back on track. But the specific stories that paint this picture do something else. These stories show God's glory—his brilliance shining all the more brilliantly when viewed against the dark backdrop of his people's sin.

The vicious cycle begins to play out in this story. In the middle of verse 12, the narrator tells us that "because they did this evil the LORD gave Eglon king of Moab power over Israel. Getting the Ammonites and Amalekites to join him, Eglon came and attacked Israel, and they took possession of the City of Palms. The Israelites were subject to Eglon king of Moab for eighteen years" (Judg. 3:12–14). It is a shock to read that Eglon took possession of the City of Palms, because the City of Palms is Jericho, the first city Israel captured under Joshua when they entered the promised land. Now that city has been recaptured, and Israel has been in bondage for eighteen years.

What is Israel to do? Verse 15 says, "Again the Israelites cried out to the LORD, and he gave them a deliverer—Ehud, a left-handed man, the son of Gera the Benjamite. The Israelites sent him with tribute to Eglon king of Moab."

All right, there are a couple details you need to know about Ehud. First, he's left-handed. That is going to be significant in the story. You have to realize that the writers of Bible stories told them in a spare, lean style. There are none of John Grisham's elaborate character descriptions—the light yellow shirt, the straw hat, the short brown hair that was half gray, and the wide bony shoulders of Rachel Lane in *The Testament*. No, biblical storytellers rarely mention that kind of stuff. When they do, it has something to do with the story line. There are no throwaway lines in Bible stories. Ehud was left-handed. That's the first detail. But second, he was from the tribe of Benjamin. Does anyone know what Benjamin means? It is the Hebrew expression "Son of my right hand." How ironic! We have a left-hander from a tribe named after the right hand. That is not what we expect, but we will see the significance soon enough.

What Ehud does next may seem innocent, but it's really an act that heightens the suspense. Verse 16 tells us, "Now Ehud had made a double-edged sword about a cubit long, which he strapped to his right thigh under his clothing." There is intrigue in this action. The sword crafted by Ehud is short. This is not the normal word for an eighteen-inch sword. Old Testament scholar Lawson Younger argues that the sword's length is only a foot long. The sword is also double-edged, literally "double-mouthed." It is not the kind you use in battle to hack someone. It is designed more for a jab and slice. Ehud straps this to his right thigh.

Ooh, that is intriguing! Since most of you do not use swords in your daily routines, you might need to think about where a warrior would normally strap his sword. Most warriors are right-handed. If you are right-handed, that sword gets strapped to your left side so you can whip it out quickly. If you strapped it to your right side, you would probably pull a few muscles trying to get it out of its sheath! What all this means is that if you ever had to be frisked in those days for a concealed weapon—before the days of metal detectors and body scanning—most guards or officers would quickly pat your left thigh to check for a weapon. Ehud straps his handcrafted, double-edged sword to his right thigh because he's left-handed. It won't get detected when he goes through airport security! So what do you think he's going to do with this sword?

Verse 17 tells us what Ehud does next: "He presented the tribute to Eglon king of Moab, who was a very fat man." Here's more description—rare stuff in Hebrew stories. And this particular description strikes me as mean. Pointing out that Eglon was a very fat man is not kind, sensitive, respectful, or socially correct. But once again, this detail will come into play in the story. The term "fat" is used often in the Old Testament to refer to fattened sheep or cattle. And guess what Eglon's name means? Eglon means "calf." So we've got a fattened calf here . . . perhaps a fattened calf ready for slaughter!

But for the moment, Ehud presents the tribute to Eglon. King Eglon and the Moabites have defeated Israel, and now they're making Israel pay a huge tax in exchange for a little peace. This Moabite king is basically practicing extortion. He's like a bully who says to a little kid, "If you don't give me a dollar, I won't let you keep walking on this sidewalk by my house." So Ehud makes another payment. But then the story takes an interesting turn. Look at verses 18–19: "After Ehud had presented the tribute, he sent on their way those who had carried it. But on reaching the stone images near Gilgal he himself went back to Eglon."

Gilgal. Does that name sound familiar? It was the place where Israel set up memorial stones to commemorate God's miracle of allowing them to cross the Jordan River when it was swollen at flood stage. The story appears in Joshua 3–4. Now, instead of memorial stones, there are stone images. The Hebrew expression used here refers to carved, sculpted stones that people worshiped. It is another sad reminder of how God's people disintegrated when they began living like their pagan neighbors. A sacred crossing has become a place of idol worship. But it is at this crossing that Ehud makes a story-changing move. Again, the text says, "he himself went back to Eglon and said, 'Your Majesty, I have a secret message for you'" (v. 19).

Oh, the power of a secret! How many times have you lured someone your way by saying, "Come here, I want to tell you a secret"? Ehud has a secret message. The Hebrew word translated "message" is a generic, ambiguous term. It refers to a word, a matter, a thing. It is like our word *something*. Something can mean just about anything! Once, one of my sons walked up to me with his hands hidden behind his back and said, "Dad, I've got something for you." So I walked up, and—*pow!*— he punched me right in the stomach. Ehud says, "Oh, King Eglon, I've got a secret something for you." And Eglon, this fat king who can't get his fill of food and life's other delights, is tantalized by this secret. Why, maybe it's an announcement of an additional gift. Maybe it's a report about a traitor in one of his subject territories. Maybe it's a bribe that will provide Eglon with more wealth. So, as verse 19 reports, "The king said to his attendants, 'Leave us!' And they all left."

Can you feel the suspense building? What is the surprise? Look at verse 20: "Ehud then approached him while he was sitting alone in the upper room of his palace"—probably an elevated throne room—"and said, 'I have a message from God for you.'" Did you catch the slight change in wording? Ehud not only has a message, he has a message from God! And here is the moment we have been anticipating, the moment at which the text has been hinting. Verse 20 continues, "As the king rose from his seat"—and it must have been a chore, given his obesity—"Ehud reached with his left hand, drew the sword from his right thigh and plunged it into the king's belly. Even the handle sank in after the blade"—and here the New International Version gets it exactly right—"and his bowels discharged. Ehud did not pull the sword out, and the fat closed in over it." That's another little detail that will soon come into play. "Then Ehud went out to the porch; he shut the doors of the upper room behind him and locked them."

All right, we are not exactly sure what verse 23 means when it says that "Ehud went out to the porch." The word translated "porch" may refer to some kind of opening, possibly a toilet drain. Apparently, Ehud has locked the doors from the inside and then escaped through this opening. Perhaps he even walked through a room where the king's guards and attendants were stationed, said good-bye, and then walked away.

What happens next seems to fall into the category that my children call "TMI"—too much information. In verse 24 we read, "After he had gone, the servants came and found the doors of the upper room locked. They said, 'He must be relieving himself in the inner room of the palace.' They waited to the point of embarrassment." You can figure out what is going on here. The king is in his throne room, and the smell makes them suspicious that he's seated on his other throne . . . relieving himself. We know it's because his bowels have discharged. Nobody wants to walk in on a king seated on his other throne. How embarrassing! "But when he did not open the doors of the room, they took a key and unlocked them. There they saw their lord fallen to the floor, dead." When the servants finally got the courage and a key to the door and opened it, they saw King Eglon reduced to a lifeless blob and a pile of human waste!

Meanwhile, verse 26 tells us, "While they waited"—and the expression suggests a long delay—"Ehud got away." It took awhile to figure out that King Eglon had been assassinated. Remember, his fat rolls had closed in over the dagger. This delay gave Ehud time to escape. By the time someone figured out what had happened, Ehud was long gone. Verse 26 continues:

> He passed by the stone images and escaped to Seirah. When he arrived there, he blew a trumpet in the hill country of Ephraim, and the Israelites went down with him from the hills, with him leading them.
> "Follow me," he ordered, "for the LORD has given Moab, your enemy, into your hands." So they followed him down and took possession of the fords of the Jordan that led to Moab; they allowed no one to cross over. At that time they struck down about ten thousand Moabites, all vigorous and strong; not one escaped. That day Moab was made subject to Israel, and the land had peace for eighty years. (vv. 26–30)

All right, who is the hero in this story? Is it Ehud? Sometimes we identify too closely with Ehud and assume that God is saying, "I will use your unique abilities to win battles when you have courage." But I do not believe the writer of the story intended for us to take it that way. Ehud is not the real hero, but he tells us who the real hero is in verse 28. It is none other than Israel's God, Yahweh! Yes, Yahweh came through and delivered his people. Yahweh gave Moab into Israel's hands. But did you notice how he did it? He did it in a rather unexpected way. There is surprise at every point in the story: A left-handed warrior from a tribe with a right-handed name. A secret message. An escape made possible by the delay caused by the smell of a king presumably going to the bathroom.

Just when the Israelites, after eighteen years, are wondering if they will ever escape domination by Moab, Yahweh delivers his people in a most surprising, most unexpected way. Who would have thought that God would ever do it that way?

When we think about God's character, we often think about his constancy, the fact that he never changes. Like the old hymn says,

> Thou changest not, Thy compassions they fail not.
> As Thou has been Thou forever wilt be.

And it's true. God's character does not change. His love, his mercy, his compassion . . . you can count on them day after day, year after year, century after century. But that does not mean God is always predictable. He is certainly not boring. No, we serve a God who delights in surprise, in the unexpected. He is a God who delivers his people in ways you never anticipate and at times that you never expect!

That's what this story is about. *God delivers his people from hopeless situations in unexpected ways.* There's mystery, intrigue, and deliverance. That's how God does it. He likes irony. He is in control of the bizarre twists and turns of life, the strange decisions and choices people make. He is sovereign. Working through the choices of human beings, God's will gets done. He accomplishes his salvation. God delivers his people from hopeless situations in unexpected ways.

Suddenly, my mind flies through Scripture, and I remember the surprising ways in which God delivered his people. Do you remember the story of Moses and the ark? Yes, Moses and the ark! Remember when the Egyptian Pharaoh ordered the execution of any baby boys born to Hebrew women? Moses's mother hid him in what the Hebrew text calls a little "ark" made of bulrushes. Pharaoh's daughter ended up finding him. She brought up Moses in Pharaoh's court where he got the education he needed for a time later in his life when he'd deliver God's people. And Pharaoh's daughter hired Moses's own mother as a nanny! She got paid to nurse her own son. How's that for a surprise!

Then there is the story of Esther. The Jews were in danger of being exterminated. An enemy named Haman had plotted their demise. But on a night when the Persian king had insomnia, he decided to pull out his royal records and read them. You would expect this to put him right back to sleep, but instead he made a discovery that led him to honor the very Jewish man that Haman wanted to execute!

Then there is the apostle Paul. Who would have thought that God's man for developing and protecting the church from its most intimidating enemy would transform from a terrorist into its greatest leader?

And then there's Jesus . . . the greatest deliverer of all. Who would have thought that God would meet the deepest needs of the human race by coming himself to earth in human form, and rather than live with royalty, would enter a poor carpenter's family? Who would have thought that God's plan for triumph included a shameful death on a cross? The gospel is the good news that God, through the death and resurrection of his Son, has delivered us from our sin! It is the ultimate deliverance, and the Ehud story anticipates it.

Quite honestly, the fact that God delivers his people from hopeless situations in unexpected ways gets me through those days when I feel like giving up. When I wonder if there's any hope for some rather hopeless situations, I remember Ehud, and Moses, and Esther, and Paul, and Jesus. And I remember how in my own life I have seen God at work delivering his people from hopeless situations in unexpected ways.

When I was a boy, my father was the director of a church-planting organization that sent a church planter and his family to a town on the Oregon coast. Not long after the church planter arrived, he received a visit from a logger named Charley. Charley pointed out that the town charter read, "There will never be a church in this town." Charley told this church planter, "You've got three months to get out, or else."

Every week Charley paid the pastor a visit and said, "You've got ten weeks left to get out." "You've got nine weeks left to get out." And the town watched. They wondered what the church planter would do. They wondered what Charley would do if the church planter did not leave. "You've got four weeks to get out." "You've got three weeks to get out." Two weeks before the deadline, Charley was killed in a logging accident. And today there is a gospel-preaching church in that town on the Oregon coast. God delivers his people from hopeless situations in unexpected ways.

A few years ago, when I pastored a church in Montana, we had a neighbor who had nothing to do with our church family. The only time he ever set foot on our property was to cuss out a kid in our youth group. This teen had pulled his little Toyota pickup in front of our neighbor's SUV.

I realized then that our neighbor's temper and his influence in our community could have a harmful effect on our ministry. Some months later, I ended up in this neighbor's home after a death in his family. To make a long story short, someone in our church gave one of the most blunt, offensive presentations of the gospel I ever heard. I thought our relationship with this guy was going to get worse. But the neighbor responded to the gospel, and today he is a leader in this church! Once again, God came through. He delivered us from a potential mess in a quite surprising way—through one of the most insensitive presentations of the gospel I have ever heard.

I can imagine the scene many centuries ago. A group of Israelite shepherds gather around a campfire, full from cheese and lentil soup. The banter increases, the laughter echoes in the canyon, the campfire crackles, and its shadows dance on the wall of the ravine. At one point someone says, "Hey, remember that story about Ehud, the left-handed guy who said, 'King Eglon, I have a secret message for you'?" Before long, the shepherds are doubling over with laughter. After the laughter subsides, there's a brief moment of silence while the firelight keeps dancing on the wall of the ravine, that moment before someone shares another story, and one of the older shepherds says, "Hmm, you never know how God is going to deliver you when you face a hopeless situation. You just never know!"

Commentary

Good sermons are often presented with strong titles. If you write a book, the title can increase the sales—or decrease them—by as much as 20 percent. People who make movies realize that a good title can get people to come to the theater. Preachers are aware of this as well. Steve Mathewson titles his sermon "The Story of the Left-Handed Assassin and the Obese King." He calls attention to that title by apologizing for using it and then apologizing for preaching from the book of Judges. He isn't really apologizing. This increases the listeners' interest. Titles are vital if you advertise your sermon in the newspaper or on a display board outside the church. Some titles stand out and others just lie there like soggy cereal. If I were glancing through the paper and saw "The Story of the Left-Handed Assassin and the Obese King" I would think, *that doesn't sound very religious*, which can be a strength.

His idea in the sermon, which the introduction points to from the very beginning, is that God delivers his people from helpless situations in unexpected ways. Having presented the idea with a series of illustrations, one about a church planter who is trying to establish his church in Oregon and another about his church back in Montana, the application to the congregation is that you never know how God is going to deliver you when you face a helpless situation. You just never know. That is the final line of the sermon and well suited to the theme of the sermon.

Interview

How do you go about preparing a sermon?

I break it down into two phases: the text phase and the sermon construction phase. In the text phase I begin with an independent study of the text, my Bible—it could be an English Bible, Hebrew Bible, Greek Bible . . . just a Bible. I used to use a legal pad and a pen with my Bible, and now it's my Bible and a word processing document. I work through the text on my own and wrestle with it before I ever look at any tools or commentaries. I do a basic inductive Bible study, making observations as I go. Toward the end of that I'll take a stab and ask, "What seems to be the main idea? How does this flow?"

Once I do that, I'll eventually get to the commentaries. I feel I'm much better prepared to interact with the commentaries after I've done my own study and my own thinking. I think it's important that I interact with them because Ephesians 4 reminds us that God has given the church pastors and teachers, and I think we need to study Scripture in community. We learn from one another. That's important. The end of that text phase is when I've settled on the exegetical idea of the passage.

Once the text phase is done, I move to the sermon construction phase. I think through how the sermon should flow and what the basic outline will be. I follow the text on that. How should this flow? Should this be more inductive or deductive? Then I'll put together an outline. I shoot for a one-page outline and then think about supporting material—illustrations or images I might use, where I'll put application, what details about the text need to be discussed. After that I still do a manuscript, either a full manuscript or, occasionally, depending on the week and time, I may just manuscript part of it, but that's important.

When do the homiletical idea and purpose come into play?

Early in the sermon construction phase, maybe before or during the outline. Sometimes I honestly am not able to improve a lot on the way I stated the exegetical idea. I guess it's kind of a fluid process. The exegetical idea may come out sounding timeless enough that it really works as a preaching idea. It's early on in the sermon construction phase where I decide how I'm going to word the idea. But even though I try to do that early on, sometimes when I'm doing the manuscript—that late, as I'm thinking through it (that's part of the benefit of doing a manuscript)—it doesn't sound quite right, so I'll work on it a little bit more. I may start at the beginning of the sermon construction phase, but it may not be in its final form. I may even change it at the end.

Why is a manuscript important?

I think it's important because it's a way of thinking through what I'm going to say, and of course this gets into preaching without notes. I do preach without notes. I find it really essential to write a manuscript so that I'm able to think through how I'm going to present things. Writing is a way of thinking. I find that having to wrestle with what I'm going to say and how I'm going to say it is part of the process. Then I can go back later and reread it. I never try to memorize a manuscript. I'll internalize it. I'm familiar enough with it that when I stand up and preach, it just comes out.

What would you tell new preachers about preaching without notes? Would you encourage them to give it a try?

I would really encourage them to give it a try. To some people it may not seem to fit their personalities. I started by preaching from a full manuscript. And the worst gaffs I ever made in messages were when I preached *with* a full manuscript. I think I was afraid of leaving things out. What

I've learned is that the details really do remember themselves. I just have to remember the big-picture things. I would tell younger preachers to give it a try. I think in this age, really trying to pursue eyeball-to-eyeball communication is good. That's the way we get a lot of our communication through the media. I also find preaching without notes to be very freeing. It may not be for everyone, but at least try it and see if it works for you.

How long does it take to prepare a sermon?

I'm going to guess sixteen to twenty hours. It's not just the number of hours, but it's having the sermon preparation process take place over time. It may only be a week, but I'd rather have, say, ten hours spread over five days (two hours a day for five days) than to have three eight-hour days (twenty-four hours). When I step away from work I've done and come back the next day, connections get made. My mind has been working on things subconsciously.

The other thing I would want to say about the sermon preparation process is to bathe it in prayer. Throughout the process I'm praying, praying for insight and also praying that I'll understand how this connects with my congregation.

As you pray through it, you're rehearsing it too?

I'll start as early as Saturday night. Then I have the advantage because I'm sleeping on it. I'll go through it again on Sunday morning. It's really important to go through it on a Saturday night.

How do you outline a narrative?

It's important to follow the contours of the story. Any good story, including Bible stories, is built upon some kind of a crisis and some kind of a resolution. I also find that helpful in trying to identify the big idea of a particular narrative. That doesn't mean point one is going to be crisis and point two is going to be resolution, but that's the starting point. Then I'll try to look for the major movements of that story. Invariably the outline will be built around crisis. Here's the problem and here's the solution or the answer.

How important are transitions in a narrative sermon?

They're huge. They help people connect ideas together. I write them out in my outline and in my manuscript.

Why choose to preach Judges?

Even though it has been neglected, it's a book I was drawn to because of the theology it contains and what it teaches about God and his relationship to people. It has something to say to culture today. Our culture has turned its back on God. That's certainly what you have going on in Judges. Judges helps us see what the consequences are for doing that and helps us see how God delivers people out of the messes that they create. Judges is a bizarre book. It's got a lot of dark stuff, and it's certainly not what a lot of people are used to hearing. But it contains profound theological messages.

Tell me about your sermon series.

I plan a sermon series anywhere from six months to two years out.

How do you determine what to include in a series?

In terms of what I choose, I would say, "Well, I'm looking at where our congregation is. What do we need?" A couple years ago I felt we really needed to go back and review the gospel and what it looks like when we flesh it out in our lives. Based on that, I chose to go through Romans. I also vary between the Old and New Testaments. I try to preach as much from the Old Testament as the New. I balance literary genres. People connect differently to the variety of literary forms found in the Bible. Some people love stories. Others want the linear, highly reasoned, tightly argued approach like you might find in Paul's letters or in the other epistles. Others are thrilled when I'm doing psalms or poetry. When I say I'm two years out, that doesn't necessarily mean I can tell you that on January 17, 2016,

I'll do this exact message. But I do know that in the winter of 2016, unless something changes, I'm planning on preaching Romans or Proverbs.

How would you describe expository preaching in your own words? What has it come to mean to you?

It's unpacking a text of Scripture so the truth is exposed and applied to the listeners.

How do you deal with authorial intent and sermon application?

My application may go in a little bit different direction than what the original writer was doing at that moment, because he was speaking to a specific audience. Maybe my listeners have different needs. But I think my applications have to align with the author's intent. I wouldn't want to preach something where I felt like if the writer of Judges saw this application he would shake his head and say, "This is not even remotely connected to what I was saying!" You'd want that writer to say, "Okay, I see what he's doing. He's speaking to a different group of listeners with a different set of issues. But he's taking the message I was trying to communicate and applying it legitimately."

Tell me about your use of Hebrew. How do you decide when to talk about the original language? Do I need to be a language shark to preach the Old Testament?

Great question! I think we have to be cautious that we don't bore people or discourage people by throwing out a lot of Greek and Hebrew. But people like insight. I'm only going to share an insight when it sheds light on the meaning of the text. Probably 95 percent of what I discover when I'm looking at the Hebrew and Greek text doesn't get mentioned, but it shapes the sermon. I don't want to convey to the people that we can't understand the Bible if we don't know Hebrew and Greek.

You don't have to be a language shark. It's helpful. It's a benefit. But many preachers don't know Hebrew. That's why we have commentaries.

Your two main illustrations come toward the end of your sermon. They are personal illustrations. Do you tend to use more personal illustrations than other kinds of illustrations?

I like to use illustrations. Over the years I have used more personal illustrations than stories about Abe Lincoln or other historical figures. People value transparency. They want to hear how the truth gets lived out in my life. They want to hear about my struggles.

Do you collect illustrations?

I do collect illustrations. This is where Haddon might disown me. In my early days I tried an illustration file. I would come up with a great story and file it under "Grace." Then, two months or a year later I'd think, "What was that story about the kid who got lost in the Upper Peninsula of Michigan? I want to use it to describe God's presence." So I'd look under "Presence of God" and it wasn't there, and I'd try to remember where I filed it. So what I've done—and it's highly unscientific but it works for me—is I have a huge illustration file and any time I find a good story or anecdote I throw it in that file. Actually, I have one for stories, one for poems, and one for more scientific things. I'll thumb through those files.

Do you use illustrations differently depending on genre?

I use fewer illustrations in narrative. A lot of my illustrations are stories. I don't want to compete with the narrative. When I'm in the epistles or in literature that's a little more didactic, I'll often use a story there to illustrate something. I may use a poem or lyrics to a song, different things depending on what I'm doing. Narrative is the one place I probably don't use many illustrations, or at least I use them differently.

Do you use media when you preach?

I used to use more media. The church I pastored previously had a midweek service that was really designed for twentysomethings, and I would preach the same message that I preached a couple times on Sunday morning, but instead of the illustrations I would often use movie clips. That seemed to work well.

I will occasionally use media in the context I have now. I don't do as much video. What I find is that even though we sometimes say a picture is worth a thousand words, it's also true that a word is worth a thousand pictures. And I think it works both ways. Sometimes we rely too heavily on visual media and it keeps us from working hard to paint a picture in the listeners' minds. That's my biggest fear. If I put a picture on the screen or use a video clip, that may help some people. But I'm afraid it may hinder my efforts to paint a picture. If I'm in Judges 4 and it talks about Mount Tabor, I'll use a picture of Mount Tabor that I took when I was in Israel or that I purchased.

I'm open to but cautious about media. The way the Old Testament prophets communicated gives us latitude for using props and other things.

What do you want to accomplish in a sermon introduction?

An introduction ought to create interest, raise a need for listening to the sermon, and orient the listeners to the text. It doesn't always have to be in that order. You've got to get people engaged and interested, but beyond that they need to see why this is useful or what the payoff is for listening.

How do you keep the story moving?

You figure out where the tension is and you play that up. I tried to do that in this sermon. The narratives in the Old Testament are pretty lean and sparse in their description. When we tell the story, maybe we can pick up on those points where the writer has condensed something or made a turn that we might miss. I try to play up that tension a bit. When we see Ehud with that sword strapped to his leg, I spent some time playing up the tension. I'm just trying to help my listeners see that this is a pretty tense situation. It's also important to add some sensory details. Biblical narrative is more lean and sparse in its descriptions as compared with Western literature where we describe characters elaborately. I'll often put in a little bit of local color so hearers get a feel for what it's like to be there and what is going on.

What were challenges in applying this sermon?

I think the big challenge, like most narrative, is that you don't have a direct command or an obvious challenge. I think a narrative works a lot more subtly. Again, I believe that Judges is a Former Prophet, so it is calling God's people to believe and behave a certain way. But I think the challenge is figuring out what that message is and its implications. And if that narrative really is saying that God delivers his people in surprising and unsuspecting ways, then I have to say, "Okay, where do I need to hear that? At what point in my struggle?" This is where I go back to Haddon's whole vision of God and the depravity factor. What's the depravity factor that's working against this? Why does the writer even have to bring this up? I told this story to make this point. What's going on? If this big idea is the answer, what is the problem?

Your central idea is crystal clear. How important is it to hammer that home? Can it be overdone?

I think it's critical that the big idea gets hammered home. I do think it can be overdone, but in my experience, it's underdone. Maybe the danger with overdone is not so much that it's overdone, but it's done in a way that's too pedantic or rigid or predictable. When I first started preaching, I would say the big idea, even at the beginning of a narrative. I cringe just thinking of what I would say: "What we're going to see this morning is that . . ." I would give people the big idea or I would say, "The main idea is . . ." Now I try to be more subtle about that. I will often use the same statement again and again, but sometimes I'll restate it. If I use the same statement, hopefully it's not in a clunky fashion. I weave it into the message so it comes out naturally. Whether they realize it or not, people are hearing it four or five times.

What advice would you give to a young preacher, and what encouragement would you give to a more seasoned preacher?

Devote ample time to preaching. Young preachers just starting out have to do that. And for veteran preachers, the temptation is to try to take some shortcuts. It's true we do get into a rhythm, and I don't think it takes a veteran preacher as much time as a newbie preacher. But the danger is for us to start cutting corners. If a primary piece of our ministry is preaching the Word of God, then we really have to be diligent and take the time to study and craft the sermon.

A second piece of advice is to prepare sermons in community. There is a dimension where it is a very "alone" process, and I think that's legitimate. But I also think we're supposed to study Scripture in community. So I encourage younger and older preachers to pull together some kind of a sermon preparation team. If somebody's in a small church and he's the only staff person, the only preacher, find some people in the congregation who love the Bible and would have an hour to meet ten days before the message, and they don't even have to do a lot of preparation. Have those people read the text through a few times. Ask them what strikes them when they hear this. What needs to be explained? What don't they buy into? What needs to be applied?

Those who are in a larger church can work with a pastoral staff.

4

The Story of the Worship Leader Who Lost His Song

Psalm 73

Patricia Batten

Subject: What do we do when we doubt God's goodness?
Complement: We seek God to gain his perspective.

Exegetical Idea: When we doubt God's goodness, we should seek God to gain his perspective.

Homiletical Idea: In God's presence, we gain a new perspective.

Purpose: As a result of preaching this sermon, I want the listener

to know that there's a difference between an earthly perspective and a godly perspective;

to know that not viewing life from God's perspective can lead to doubt in God, which is a tragedy of faith;

to engage in corporate worship as a good place to gain God's perspective;

to know that God has a plan for both the godly and the wicked.

I love stories. And I love a story within a story. This morning I want to tell you a story. It's a story from the Bible, a man's faith story. I want to tell you his story because his story might just be your story. It's

Patricia Batten is part of the preaching team at Hope Community Church in Newburyport, Massachusetts. She is also a ranked adjunct associate professor of preaching at Gordon-Conwell Theological Seminary in Hamilton, Massachusetts. Pat serves as a preaching mentor for Christian University Globalnet (CUGN). She does pulpit supply in churches in her area and speaks at women's retreats and conferences across the country.

the story of a man who doubted God's goodness. He lived three thousand years ago. He lived in a different time and a different place, but I think that if you've ever doubted God's goodness, then his story really could be your story. So this is the story of Asaph.

When Asaph was a little boy in the tribe of Levi, he grew up hearing the stories of his people Israel and what God had done for them. Do you remember the stories of your youth? You believed them, didn't you? Well, Asaph heard all about God—how God led the Israelites out of captivity in Egypt, how God parted the sea and gave to Moses the Ten Commandments. Asaph grew up learning about Abraham and the covenant that God made with the father of the Jewish people. But I bet one of Asaph's favorite bedtime stories was the one about the ark. You know how kids don't want a new bedtime story; they want their *favorite* story. "Daddy, tell me a story about the ark." Asaph grew up hearing stories about the ark—not Noah's ark . . . the ark of the covenant.

It must have been one of the most mysterious objects for a little boy or girl to imagine. Even today, thousands of years later, explorers and adventurers are mystified by the ark of the covenant. Indiana Jones searched for it in *Raiders of the Lost Ark*. I mean, just think of it, the Bible tells us that the ark was the place where YHWH dwelt. God himself was enthroned between two golden cherubim, and inside the ark were found those items that represented the Exodus: Aaron's budding staff, a piece of the manna that God rained down from heaven, and of course, the Ten Commandments. The ark of the covenant—every child's dream story. "Mom, Dad, tell me the story about the ark."

But when Asaph was a boy, the ark was in and out of enemy hands. It was guarded by priests and armies who did not fear the Lord. It fell into the hands of Israel's enemy, the Philistines. They figured that if they caught the ark, then they'd cripple Israel's God. So they brought the ark back to one of their towns and placed it in one of their temples—right next to one of their gods called Dagon. Wouldn't you know it, the next morning the Philistines went into the temple to find Dagon facedown in front of the ark of the covenant with his head and arms broken off. Not only that, but the town was plagued by devastating diseases. The townspeople wanted that ark out of their sight. So after some maneuvering, the ark ended up back in Israel, in someone's home—Abinidab, who lived on a hill in Kiriath Jearim. The ark rested there for twenty years. Twenty years. And young Asaph grew up.

So the ark rested for twenty years, until David came along. Asaph knew right off that there was something different about David. He inspired people. There was something about David that made people rally about him. He had a way of calling the people back to worshiping God.

Asaph remembered that David got some men together and he had them move the ark. He wanted to bring it to Jerusalem, where it belonged. But when they got as far as Kidon's threshing floor, one of the oxen that was helping to carry the ark stumbled—so Uzzah reached out his hand to steady the ark and instantly he was struck down. The joy of that day was immediately wiped away with the death of a friend. Asaph would never forget the blow of that day. Why? Why did it happen? And the ark remained at the household of Obed-Edom for about three months until David got organized.

David said, "Let's try this again. But we'll do it right this time. This time, the Levites—and the Levites only—will carry the ark, as God told Moses so many years before. Let's have singers and dancers and musicians lead the procession in worship." Asaph remembered that day well. You see, Asaph was a Levite and a gifted musician—a gifted percussionist.

Can you even imagine it? The ark of the covenant! And Asaph was leading the procession with his music. Side by side with King David. What a day! What a moment! And of course you know how things progress. Asaph eventually landed a job as one of David's chief worship leaders. And David gave Asaph a song—one of the first songs Asaph got from David. You can read it in 1 Chronicles 16:8–36. It's a song of praise and thanksgiving to God. Asaph could never forget that day. His song was full of joy. But by the time we get to Psalm 73, it looks as though Asaph has changed his tune—from one of delight in God to doubt in God.

So why did Asaph change his tune? What happened? Asaph changed his tune because he looked around and he saw that wicked people prosper and godly people suffer. Just look at how Asaph begins this psalm: "Surely God is good to Israel, to those who are pure in heart" (v. 1). Sounds good. But I can't help wondering if there isn't a hint of sarcasm in Asaph's voice: "Oh yeah, God's real good to the pure in heart. God's real good to the faithful." Asaph doesn't buy it. He's at the point in his life where he doesn't even believe God is good. Asaph doubts God's goodness because he sees the wicked prosper and the godly suffer. And that's what has turned his delight in God to doubt.

Maybe you've had your own Psalm 73 moments when you've doubted God's goodness. We'd never admit it here, in this place . . . but we've sat in these pews week after week praising and thanking God, and has there ever been a Sunday when you've said to yourself, "I don't know if I believe this anymore. God's goodness? Not in my life!"

I suppose it's easy to doubt God's goodness to the pure in heart. Just look at the impure in heart. Look at how the wicked prosper. Look at some of the people who don't acknowledge God. For many of them, life is a breeze. They sail on the carefree winds of their own hot air and arrogance. No worries of money or health. They live by the motto "Me first, you last." They get things done by way of force and oppression, and God does nothing. He allows it. Whether it's a dictator oppressing a nation or an oppressive boss dictating your workload and your paycheck—there are people out there who don't acknowledge God, yet they live what seems to be the good life. But for so many who follow God, the wind never seems to be at their backs. Their worries are too many and their paychecks too small. They don't sail in carefree winds. In fact, they don't even enjoy the ride. They just hope they make it back to shore.

Seeing the way the world really works can make any person of faith have doubts. You know what I mean. You're out for your morning walk or jog, and you hear the smooth roar of an engine approaching. You recognize the sound. It's a Hummer, an H2, and you know who's behind the wheel. He's a local businessman who has a well-deserved reputation for playing dirty. He's not running on the side of the road. He's just come from the club. He's worked out with state-of-the-art equipment. He has a personal trainer. He's already had a steam bath and a massage, and as he whizzes by you he's sipping his iced single venti mocha, no whip. He's on his way to the golf course. He speeds by you, and you're forced off the narrow road into the bushes. But not only that—the roads have been wet from the rain, and he never bothers to slow down as he flies through a puddle. You're left in the bushes like a drowned rat.

Seeing the way the world really works can make any person of faith have doubts. When we see the way the wicked prosper, it can make us doubt God's goodness, and that was true for Asaph.

The tune that once praised the goodness of God now doubted. And you can see how doubt crept in. Asaph looked around and saw wicked people prospering and godly people suffering. As a worship leader, Asaph met a whole lot of people over the course of the years. He worked with hundreds of people—singers, instrumentalists, dancers. He wrote and learned music for the worship of God. When people came to the tabernacle, a cacophony of voices echoed through the timbers, shouting and singing praises to God Almighty. So Asaph got to know a lot of people. He was there in their times of rejoicing and he was there in their times of sorrow. But lately, as Asaph headed to work, cymbals in hand, he didn't feel like making music. Because as he headed down the dusty roads of Jerusalem, all he could see was grief. His friend Becky, she was barren. She desperately wanted to have children. In that culture, she *needed* to have children. But she had none. Maybe there was Asaph's neighbor, Jacob, whose house had been robbed and vandalized. Or perhaps only days before a close colleague was slandered at the city gate, his reputation ruined. His path clouded by dust and his mind dusted with doubt, Asaph wondered, "Where is God?" And maybe you've wondered that same question, "Where is God?"

Now when Asaph made his way to work he didn't have that spring in his step. He didn't have that song in his heart. You remember that excitement that came with a new job. You bought into the company vision; you were going to make a difference. But Asaph doesn't buy that line anymore. He's not interested in rehearsing the singers, practicing with the musicians, and choreographing the dancers for the worship service. Why bother with worship? God doesn't care about his people anyway. I mean, just look around. There seems to be no special protection for God's people. God doesn't discriminate between those who love him and those who hate him. Just look at the way Asaph begins his song: "Surely God is good to Israel, to those who are pure in heart." I detect sarcasm in Asaph's voice. God says he's good to Israel, to the pure in heart. God is supposed to be good to these people. But it actually looks as though the ungodly are better off. Asaph says that he envied the arrogant when he saw the prosperity of the wicked:

> They have no struggles;
>   their bodies are healthy and strong.
> They are free from common human burdens;
>   they are not plagued by human ills.
> Therefore pride is their necklace;
>   they clothe themselves with violence.

From their callous hearts comes iniquity;
  their evil imaginations have no limits.
They scoff, and speak with malice;
  with arrogance they threaten oppression.
Their mouths lay claim to heaven,
  and their tongues take possession of the earth.
Therefore their people turn to them
  and drink up waters in abundance.
They say, "How would God know?
  Does the Most High know anything?"
This is what the wicked are like—
  always free of care, they go on amassing wealth.
Surely in vain I have kept my heart pure
  and have washed my hands in innocence. (vv. 4–13)

Have you ever thought those words? Maybe you were afraid to say them out loud, so they were simply a shadow lingering in the back of your mind. Have you ever thought that you were a Christian in vain? Have you ever thought you followed God's will for no good reason at all? When we sign up for something, we expect something out of it, don't we? We sign on to God—we expect his protection, his love. But when we look around us, it seems as though the bad guys have more benefits from God than the good guys.

These thoughts plagued Asaph's mind—with each step he took, each chorus he conducted. What happens when the worship leader doesn't have the heart for worship? He fakes it. Have you ever faked something? Maybe you've faked a smile. Maybe you've faked enjoying the company of a co-worker. Maybe you've faked your way through school and the business world. Maybe you've faked your love for a spouse. Maybe you're faking your way through life, always wondering when someone will find out who you really are. But have you ever faked worship? Faking something wears on a person, and Asaph was getting tired. Maybe you are too. Maybe like Asaph you're just bubbling inside. You've been at a low boil, but now you're ready to explode. You're ready to stand up and shout with Asaph, "Yeah, why *do* the wicked prosper? God does not care about his people! Just look around!"

So go ahead, Asaph . . . tell the choir, tell the dancers, tell the musicians what you're feeling. Let it all out. God doesn't care—just look at the way the wicked prosper!

But Asaph couldn't do it. He couldn't tell the congregation that God was not good. God's people were standing before him; God's people wanting to hear and experience God. The words wouldn't come out. Maybe it was looking into the eyes of a hungry congregation . . . hungry for a touch from God Almighty. Maybe it was being in the midst of God's people worshiping God. Asaph knew what it was. Those words swelled in his throat, and it wasn't until he realized he was in God's presence that he was able to choke them back down: "If I had spoken out like that, I would have betrayed your children. When I tried to understand all this, it troubled me deeply till I entered the sanctuary of God; then I understood their final destiny" (vv. 15–17).

It's in God's presence that we get a changed perspective. When we truly worship God and seek his perspective, he changes the way we see things. He shows us the truth about life. And given the world around us, sometimes it's hard to focus on God and seek his perspective in times of doubt.

Asaph changes in some way when he enters the sanctuary of God. This is the turning point of the entire psalm. But you may be wondering, wasn't Asaph always in the sanctuary of God? He worked there! Asaph was always in church. Wasn't he always in God's presence? Asaph was in the tabernacle, but he was far from God. Maybe you know what that feels like—you're close to the church but far from God. That's how doubt works; it draws us away from God and limits our perspective. The more we doubt, the less we want to go to God. And the more we doubt, the more our eyes are turned away from God's goodness and toward the evils of the world. It's easy to take our eyes off of God when life around us can be so dark, but being in God's presence involves focusing on God and his view of things.

Any pilot knows the story of Jimmie Doolittle. In 1929, Doolittle became the first aviator to take off, fly a fixed course, and land a plane using instruments alone. Despite a blacked-out windshield, Doolittle was able to safely land his aircraft. Doolittle could see nothing except his instruments. His perspective came from one place and one place only. When everything else around him was dark and black, Doolittle kept his eyes focused on his compass. Darkness surrounded him, but he knew that when he was losing perspective—when he was doubting the compass—all he needed to do was focus on the guide.

It's in God's presence that we get a focused perspective. And only one who has God's perspective, who has been in God's presence, knows that

God is the good and only guide. Only one whose perspective has been realigned in God's presence can say with Asaph, "Yet I am always with you; you hold me by my right hand. You guide me with your counsel, and afterward you will take me into glory. Whom have I in heaven but you? And earth has nothing I desire besides you. My flesh and my heart may fail, but God is the strength of my heart and my portion forever" (vv. 23–26). Being in God's presence means putting our eyes on him—no matter what the outside circumstances—and gaining his perspective.

A good place to focus on God is right here in church. When we're in God's presence in the midst of his people, we are changed. When we're surrounded by those whose faith is strong in spite of things that are difficult to understand; when we're surrounded by people who have gone through the doubts and still believe in a good and gracious God, we are changed. You can be in the presence of God anywhere, but being in God's presence in the midst of God's people—it's in that unique environment that our perspective can really be realigned and adjusted to God's. We're reminded of his Word, we're encouraged by other believers, we're brought to the very throne of God through prayer, and we bow beneath the cross of the One who died for us. It's in God's presence that we get a changed perspective.

This doesn't mean that our circumstances will change, but the way we see them will change. In God's presence we'll be reminded that we have been foolish to doubt God's goodness—because he has ordained an end for the wicked. After Asaph has been in God's presence and has been given a new perspective, he is able to say, "Surely you place them on slippery ground; you cast them down to ruin. How suddenly are they destroyed, completely swept away by terrors! They are like a dream when one awakes; when you arise, Lord, you will despise them as fantasies" (vv. 18–20). Not only has God ordained an end for the wicked, but he's promised to sustain his people.

On July 16, 1999, John Kennedy Jr.; his wife, Carolyn Bessette-Kennedy; and her sister, Lauren Bessette, were approaching Martha's Vineyard in Kennedy's Piper Saratoga. The weather forecast that Kennedy got from the internet about two hours before his flight offered no warning of the haze that hung over his route from New Jersey to Martha's Vineyard. The forecast was for good visual flying conditions with visibility of six to eight miles.

When his plane was recovered from the floor of the Atlantic Ocean, it was determined that there were no mechanical failures. Experts have concluded that Kennedy might have become disoriented while flying over the ocean on a nearly moonless night in thick haze. Kennedy had more than three hundred hours of flying time. However, pilots said that three hundred hours would have left Kennedy at an experience level when pilots often become overconfident and are not sufficiently seasoned to recognize dangerous situations. Kennedy lost perspective. Kennedy defaulted to his own instincts. His mechanical compass was in good working condition; it had been checked only days before the deadly flight. But Kennedy began to doubt his instruments. His head was telling him one thing but his instruments were saying another, and Kennedy was completely off kilter. Kennedy's perspective was flawed. He completely lost his way and it cost him his life and the lives of his passengers. Losing perspective is tragic in flight, and it's tragic in faith. Doubting the compass—the guide—will give you a flawed perspective.

The only way to regain proper perspective is to go back to the compass—to go back to the guide—even when what you see around you doesn't seem to match the guide. That's what Asaph did. Verse 17 tells us that he went into the sanctuary of God and his perspective changed. In the midst of tragic doubt, going back to the compass, to your guiding force, is sometimes the hardest thing to do, but it's the only thing to do when doubt obscures perspective. It's in God's presence that we get a changed perspective.

Commentary

Everybody doubts. Your preacher doubts and you doubt. Atheists doubt. Believers doubt. This sermon by Pat Batten deals with doubt, and it is also a story. On two fronts it appeals to people's interest: it is a popular subject and an interesting way to communicate it. Psalm 73, the passage on which Batten bases her sermon, is itself a story. Any thoughtful person can identify with a leader in the church who wonders if the whole thing is true. The introduction begins back in the ancient world, but it is as up to date as the questions people in the pew face today.

Interview

How do you go about preparing to preach?

There are two phases to my sermon prep: exegetical and homiletical. I don't sit down with Haddon's ten stages on my desk every week and use them like a checklist. But I do think about the stages, just not in a formal kind of way.

During the exegetical phase, I study the passage. I read different translations, and while I read, I write down all of my questions. The questions are helpful because when I go to the commentaries, I know what I'm looking for.

Once I've got the subject/complement and the author's flow of thought, I try to connect the passage to my audience. Now I'm in the homiletical phase. I determine how to communicate this idea to a modern audience, to my audience in particular.

I spend a lot of time organizing my thoughts, getting a flow. I define the major moves in my sermon and fill in an outline. I try to make it pretty simple. For this sermon, there were two major moves: (1) We doubt God's goodness when we see wicked people prosper and godly people suffer. (2) In God's presence, we gain a new perspective. I work at connecting those thoughts through a transition. In this sermon, the transition comes when Asaph says, "If I had spoken out like that, I would have betrayed your children." The doubting God part (the problem) is over, and now we move on to the solution (in God's presence we get a new perspective). That's how it flows in the passage as well.

Tell me about your conclusion.

I wasn't sure if I should end with a negative illustration. Figuring out how to conclude isn't as easy as it seems. The mood of this sermon is somber, and the closing illustration (John Kennedy Jr.) has a lot to do with that. I probably spend the least amount of time on my conclusions. I don't intend to do things that way, but that's just how it works out. Having said that, conclusions are pretty important. That's what people leave with—it's the last thing you say. That's what they remember.

I use two illustrations to show what seeking God's perspective is like. One is a positive example, the other is a negative example. I wanted to show that getting our perspective from someplace other than God can be tragic in faith.

Tell me about illustrations. Do you collect them and file them?

I'm always on the lookout for illustrations. I went through my illustration file a few years ago, and I ended up discarding an enormous amount of it. It just wasn't relevant. Now I have more of a story folder. I save stories. I get a bunch of stories from National Public Radio. I also use resources from the National Storytelling Network (storynet.org) and the National Storytelling Festival (storytellingcenter.net). I'll even write my own stories for sermons. I also listen to other preachers and how they use illustrations. Andy Stanley and Tim Keller are on my iPod right now.

My husband is a great resource for illustrations. He has a different perspective, and he interacts with different people. He cuts things out of sections of the newspaper that I never read; he tells me what does and doesn't interest somebody like him. He reminds me that Gostkowski is the Patriot's kicker and Gronkowski is the tight end.

The thing about illustrations is that it's more about being able to spot them. It's having an illustration outlook. They're everywhere. You just need eyes to see them.

Right now I have three small kids at home, and if I'm honest with myself, my illustrations are often mom-centered. I have to be careful of that. We have a lot of parents with young children in our church, but there are many other people sitting in the congregation too. I can't ignore them, and I don't want to ignore them. But it is challenging to get outside your own little world.

Do you use notes when you preach?

No, I don't use notes. I made that commitment early on for two reasons. The first has to do with eye contact. The sermon is more of a conversation when you look at people. There's an authenticity that comes through when you look people in the eye. You can read them, gauge their reaction. Are they tracking with you?

The second reason has to do with clarity. When I can't make my transitions, it means there's something wrong with what I've written. When I can't remember what comes next, it's not my memory; it's that it wasn't written clearly to begin with. A good sermon remembers itself. I've heard Haddon say that many times, and I've found it to be true.

Why do you write a manuscript as well as an outline?

I write a manuscript because it helps me to think through wording.

What was the challenge in preaching this particular psalm?

Building the tension to verse 17, the climax of the psalm. Sticking with the problem and getting people to say, "Yeah, life is like that . . . and like Asaph, I've been on the edge of faith." They need to identify with Asaph: "Surely in vain I have kept my heart pure and have washed my hands in innocence" (v. 13). But then I want them to realize that doubting God's goodness is a dangerous place to be, and I want them to see there's a way out of that doubt.

I want to show what's at risk if this idea is not lived out in one's life. In Psalm 73, the risk is that doubting God's goodness is a tragedy of faith. Your life perspective is warped when you doubt God's goodness. Gaining God's perspective is *that* important. If the congregation doesn't know what's at risk or doesn't care about what's at risk, then the idea isn't worth their time and attention. I think showing the risk helps with application. The risk is so great that the listener will take part in figuring out how the idea applies to his or her life.

I also really used my imagination. I spent a lot of time building Asaph's story. I wanted the congregation to picture him walking along the road, shoulders slumped . . . a guy who is completely confused by what he sees in the world. We don't know a lot about him. I filled in the details, and while I don't think I went too far, I do worry about that sometimes.

How does a preacher use imagination with skill?

John Burroughs said, "To treat your facts with imagination is one thing, but to imagine your facts is another." You have to keep your imagination tied to the text. I wanted people to go on a journey with Asaph. I don't think we all of a sudden doubt God's goodness. It happens over time. Over the course of time Asaph's perspective changed. He was focused less on God and more on the world around him. I tried to fill in what that might have looked like for him and for us.

What advice would you give to a young preacher?

Make a commitment to expository preaching. That kind of commitment comes at a cost. You need to know that up front. There are a million things to do in ministry, and people in your congregation may want you to focus on the things that most interest them. But the preacher has to prioritize. Make expository preaching your priority.

I kept an index card on my desk with Haddon's "Commitments to Expository Preaching." I took those commitments seriously:

- Believe that the Bible is the Word of God.
- Believe that all of Scripture is profitable.
- Commit to a "Thus saith the Lord" view of preaching.
- Commit to hard thinking.
- Commit to authorial intent.
- Commit to relevance.

I had a group of people who prayed for me to keep those commitments.

I'd also say, be enthusiastic about preaching. If we really believe God's Word changes lives, then we'll have a little pep when we preach his Word. Be alert and engaged.

Any advice you'd give to a more seasoned preacher?

Be an expository preacher! If you're not already, give it a try. Take a look at your sermons and determine where you want to improve. Maybe it's working on a central idea—that's essential to authorial intent and also to clarity. Or maybe it's working on gestures, introductions, conclusions, transitions, or preaching without notes. Pick something and take several months to focus on it in your preaching. Be a lifelong learner in terms of preaching.

Any advice for women preachers in particular?

In addition to the above, concentrate on using the lower registers of your voice. Nobody wants to hear a screechy woman; that really gets to people. You don't have to sound like a man, but just try to use variety in your voice, especially those lower octaves. I practice using the lower register of my voice when I read to my kids.

It's also okay to smile. Don't smile constantly, but it's okay to smile. People respond kindly to a smile. It shows warmth.

I'm also grateful that I have a spouse who is honest with me about my preaching—things I do well and things that need improvement. I trust his judgment. Find a person or a small group of people who will be honest with you about your sermon. Not a compliment club, but people who can talk honestly about the message and the way it comes across. Or take time yourself to think critically about your preaching.

Is there anything you'd do differently in this sermon?

Yes. I think it's too long. And even though it's too long, there were still things I didn't take time to develop, like verses 18–20 and verse 27. I do think the thrust of the psalm is in the middle, in verse 17. It's not about *how* God will deal with the wicked in terms of the particulars. It's about gaining God's perspective in a world where evil abounds. But even so, people in the pew may be left with questions about that. They like to know the particulars.

5

Sounds That Make a Noise

Proverbs 22:1

SID BUZZELL

I am certainly honored by this opportunity to talk with you graduates and your parents tonight. It's a privilege to give this parting word to you after your four years of hard work. Tomorrow you will receive the payoff. You will officially be college graduates. It's a payoff for your hard work here, but it's really more of a send-off to the next phase of life, isn't it? We know we will be hearing about you as the years go by and you make your mark on the world. You've asked me to speak at your final banquet at CCU as a representative of my colleagues who have been your teachers. They each care deeply about you and your future, and we all want God's best plans to be fulfilled for you. It's hard to know what to say on such an occasion. To say something significant but not corny or slushy is a tough balance to find.

To avoid crossing that line, I'm just going to talk with you about noise. I want to explore some sounds. Life is full of human noises. We are surrounded by sounds that we make. We hear sighs and grunts and burps. We hear humming and ums and ahs. In my eight o'clock classes I hear yawns and heavy breathing and some occasional snoring. Sounds. Noises. They are part of who we are, aren't they?

Let me make some sounds for you. These are just noises . . . sounds that I make with my vocal cords. Some will be nonsense—like Perciwertz . . .

Sid Buzzell is dean of theology and professor of biblical exposition and leadership at Colorado Christian University in Lakewood, Colorado. He's spent twenty years as a seminary professor and thirteen years as a pastor. Dr. Buzzell speaks at conferences throughout the country.

or Likflome . . . or Moliwomp. Just noises. Others will make some sense. Here are some sounds, some noises.

Buddha, Jesus, Mohammed
Bush, Kerry
Michael, Jordan, Jackson
Washington, Adams, Jefferson
Mars, Pluto, Venus
Gibson, Aston, Nicholson
Freddy & Jason, Hannibal Lecter
McVeigh, bin Laden, Columbine
Elway, Lance Armstrong, Kobe
Hitler, Stalin, Pol Pot
Mandela, Mugabe, Mbeki
Churchill, Thatcher, Blair
Hillary, Laura, Barbara
Denver, Lakewood, Boulder
Beethoven, Elvis, Pavarotti

Noises and sounds. That's really all they are—mechanically and physiologically no different than the sounds Perciwertz, Likflome, or Moliwomp. No different, that is, until you attach meaning to them. I can give you a tour of our universe, of history, and of current events with nothing more than noises like these . . . just sounds. I can generate joy or sadness or rage in you with these noises, these sounds to which you attach meaning.

Most likely some of these sounds produced a little smile or a smirk. If you lingered over some of these sounds for a few moments, they would generate memories of wins or losses, of happy or sad moments. You would feel pride or shame or disgust. Envy or jealousy may start to percolate out of you—or admiration and awe. The response you feel to some of these sounds will be with you for life. They produce almost universal responses. Just about anyone who hears them will have similar reactions. The power these sounds have on us is amazing.

That's why Israel's brilliant sage instructed his students to treat one specific sound with great care. He was vitally concerned about this particular sound and wanted his students to share that concern. There is a crucial principle he wanted to pass on about a particular noise people hear, and the principle is so important to this wise teacher that he didn't just pass it on as a bit of advice. Solomon took time and thought to craft his counsel into a carefully constructed proverb that would force his listeners to engage his idea with their best thinking.

We find Solomon's essential piece of wisdom about this crucial sound in Proverbs 22:1.

> A good name is more desirable than great riches;
>   to be esteemed is better than silver or gold.

Think about that proverb for a little bit. Most of us get into a rhythm when we read the book of Proverbs. We tend to read by chapters and verses, and we plow through these statements like we're reading a piece of narrative. So we miss the writer's point because you can't just *read* a proverb. You have to *think* a proverb. You have to *work* a proverb. These statements were carefully constructed to force our minds to wrestle with the ideas. You see, truth discovered is more powerful than truth told. The proverbs bury their meaning just below the surface so that we have to work their meaning out of them. When we discover that truth, it is *our* truth. *We found it.* Jesus's parables are like that too. The unengaged mind will miss his point. But when we discover the point of a parable or a proverb, we have more ownership of it. So work with me on this for a few minutes. Its point will at many times in your life shape the nature and quality of formative, life-changing decisions.

Proverbs 22:1 is one of the easier proverbs to translate, but its challenge to our thinking is still there. It doesn't so much challenge us to find its meaning, but it challenges us to figure out if its meaning is valid and how it applies to our daily living. What it says is easy to discover compared to some other parables. Where we have to engage our finest thinking is in understanding how we use it. Let's work with this thing for a few minutes.

First, let's make sure we're clear about what the proverb actually says. There are two lines, like most proverbs. To read Hebrew poetry you have to see how the lines work together to produce the writer's meaning. In this proverb, the writer makes almost the same point in each line. Here's the first line: "A good name is more desirable than great riches."

Okay, got that one? You thought this was going to be hard. Now he makes essentially the same point in the second line: "to be esteemed is better than silver or gold."

> A good name is more desirable than great riches;
> to be esteemed is better than silver or gold.

You notice that both lines have a point of comparison, a baseline object with which something else is compared. In the first line the point of comparison is "great riches." He's going to compare something with that desire. Great riches is something most of us can get excited about.

In the second line the point of comparison is "silver or gold." Anyone up for those? I know you've just finished college only because you have this passionate desire to learn. But somewhere in your mind you also hope you will get a better-paying job as a result. I know some of you business majors are salivating, but most of us from the School of Theology get pretty excited about great wealth too.

So Solomon set the standard very high. Great wealth and silver and gold are things most of us dream about. Other proverbs tell us that wealth and money are valuable, useful, and desirable things. When you read the proverbs you discover that wealth, silver, and gold are evidence of wisdom. They give their owner power and influence. They open the door to pleasurable objects and experiences. They provide security and peace of mind. They provide evidence for us that Job, Abraham, and Jacob, for instance, received God's favor. So the sage laid down a basis of comparison that is tough to beat.

The second thing each line contains is a subject that Solomon is comparing to these highly desirable standards. In the first line it's "a good name." He has compared a good name to great wealth. In the second line it's "to be esteemed." He compares esteem or a good reputation with silver and gold. So he's comparing a good name with great wealth, and he's comparing a good reputation with silver and gold.

And then third, both lines express a specific *type* of comparison. How does a good name compare with great wealth, and how does a good reputation compare with silver and gold? In the first line, he says that one thing is "more desirable" than the other, and in the second line he says that one thing is "better than" the other.

So we have a good name and we have a good reputation, and they are being compared with great wealth and with silver and gold. Now here's where the proverbial nature of the statement starts to work. We have to wrestle with this idea a bit because the nature of the comparison, while it sounds neat and holy and biblical, is hard to swallow. It's what we would expect in church or at a banquet for seniors graduating from a Christian university, but it is—to most people—patent nonsense.

The comparison says that a good name is *more* desirable than great wealth, and it says that a good reputation is *better than* silver or gold.

Are you kidding me? Does he really mean that? And as soon as you ask that question, the sage who wrote the proverb says, "Gotcha!" Because for the proverb to work, you're supposed to wrestle with this idea. That's how proverbs operate. Now some proverbs engage our mind because it's tough to figure out what they mean. Proverbs 27:21 is like that: "The crucible for silver, the furnace for gold; and a man by his praise." We say, "Huh? What on earth does that mean?" Or there's Proverbs 26:17, "Like one who takes a dog by the ears is he who passes by and meddles with strife not belonging to him" (author's translation). And again we ask, "What's this guy been smoking? You gotta be high on *something* if that makes any sense to you." In proverbs like these, our mind is engaged because we're working first to figure out what on earth the proverb is saying. Only then can we wrestle with how it works in our life.

In this proverb our wrestling isn't with what the statements mean, but with their validity. Their meaning isn't hard to figure out.

> A good name is more desirable than great riches;
> to be esteemed is better than silver or gold.

But the honest mind asks, "Can this be true?"

Do you honestly believe that "a good name is more desirable than great riches"?

Can we genuinely accept the idea that "to be esteemed is better than silver or gold"?

When I'm all dressed up and speaking to nice Christian folks like us, I wouldn't dare question a proverb like this. Tidy people of God just don't do that. But I'm not always all dressed up and speaking to nice Christian people at graduation banquets. I live in a real world that would laugh at this statement all the way to the bank.

A few weeks ago Jeanette and I were in California visiting our son Chris. He is a builder and an artist, and he was working as a subcontractor on a thirty-million-dollar house in Malibu. He had just finished building some decorative walls and a fountain on that project, and he wanted to show us his work. We went upstairs to the master bedroom, which was all glass on three sides. When you stood where the bed was going to be, all you could see was ocean. It was truly breathtaking. Amazing. Genuinely awe-inspiring. That whole property, that whole house was so magnificent. I was wondering what I would have to do to live in a place like that. I can't be a rock star or a professional basketball player, so maybe I could sell drugs? Rob banks? Start a Ponzi scheme?

I have to tell you that at that moment, I wasn't thinking, "Well, I can't buy this place, but at least I have a good reputation" or "I can't afford to build a house like this, but I don't care, I have a good name. I'll just take my good name and my good reputation to the real estate office and see what oceanfront neighborhood that gets me into."

I hate to admit it to you, but at that moment this proverb didn't imme-diately spring to mind. My desire to live in a thirty-million-dollar house like that loomed large in my mind. But when the dust settled and I had some time to think about it, this proverb—Proverbs 22:1—*did* come to my mind. And that's when I decided it would be a good topic for our conversation this evening.

And I wanted to talk about it because Solomon wanted his students—including you and me—to wrestle with this crucial question of what our name is worth to us. How valuable—really, honestly—is our reputation? And what is the price for which we'll sell either of those things? Because in many ways and at many times the opportunity is there to sell out. Some-times it's silver and gold, sometimes it's sex, sometimes it's laziness or pleasure. Whatever the bargaining chip, the wisdom teacher says, "It ain't worth it to sell your name or your reputation, no matter what the price."

We played with some sounds before. Some noises generated memories, feelings, thoughts, ideas. Some responses were positive and some negative. Some of those noises challenge us to greatness and some serve as warnings to avoid destruction. Names are powerful sounds, aren't they? Some names have come to personify admiration or disgust to just about anyone who hears them. Sounds like Jesus or John, or sounds like Jezebel or Judas. Just the sounds generate feelings and attitudes.

I could make some other noises, like Jim or Sally or Fred. Names like Alice, Bill, Joe. Some of these sounds have personal and powerful and individual memories for each of us. We have our own private memories of our first love, or of the creep who dumped us after a few dates; of best friends, or of the person who bullied us or who took the lead role in the play or the solo at the concert that we so much wanted. Or the coach who stood up for you, or the teacher who helped you rewrite the paper. Some of these sounds represent the person who cheated you out of your savings or who was trying to break up your closest friendship. Some of these sounds will represent your spouse, your children, your dearest lifelong friends. Sounds that are names are powerful things. Noises that bring people to our mind carry lots of baggage—for good or for evil, for happiness or for devastation.

Solomon was well aware of the power of names when he wrote this bit of advice. He was David's son, and so he was familiar with the power of names. His father earned a name that was powerful on human lips *and* on God's heart. Jesus himself sometimes goes by the name "Son of David" because of the signal David's name gave to those in Israel who heard it. Names are powerful things. People often summarize David's history very simply by linking it with two sounds: David—and Goliath. David—and Bathsheba. David's most heroic and most tragic moments are summarized by simple sounds that represent the best and worst moments of his life. So not only does a person's own name matter, but the names a person is associated with have great power.

The point is that names matter. Names count. Names open and close doors.

Reputations matter. Reputations count. Reputations open and close doors.

> A good name is more desirable than great riches;
> to be esteemed is better than silver or gold.

Now that we see how this proverb works and what it's about, we ask, "So what?" I get the idea that my name is of more value to me than great wealth and that having a sterling reputation matters more than having silver or gold. So what should I do about that? In the tradition of working with proverbs, I pondered that very question for a while. Before looking in other places for answers to the questions these proverbs raise, we should first look for answers that Proverbs itself offers. Looking at what else Proverbs said about the topics of names and reputations and wealth and money, I generated quite a list of possible applications for this particular proverb. But since you're all going to walk out of here in about ten minutes, I had to select just a few that were most appropriate to this group and this occasion. However, don't stop thinking about this proverb after my talk is over, and don't conclude that the two suggestions I'm going to present are the best two this proverb has to offer. But I do want to start the process of thinking about how we should respond to this magnificent piece of wisdom with at least two responses.

Let's explore two implications that grow out of these lines. One is obvious, and the other isn't quite so obvious. One is the default application of the proverb, and the other is the application Solomon intended. First is the more obvious default application, that we should avoid doing things that will give us a bad name and a tarnished reputation. An implication of this proverb is that we don't want to sully our name or trash our reputation. That sounds too obvious to mention, but reality tells us that millions of people have not seen that seemingly obvious fact. Although it sounds like common sense, the old saw that there is nothing as uncommon as common sense is validated once again.

All through the book of Proverbs we are taught to avoid actions and attitudes that give us the name and reputation of the fool . . . or the wicked, or the sluggard, or the unfaithful and undisciplined. A good name is more valuable than great wealth, and esteem is more to be desired than silver and gold. So the proverb implies that just as we would not leave our checkbook on a seat at the airport, or intentionally invest in a losing stock, or lend money to a known crook, so we would not carelessly leave our name or our reputation open to destruction by being moronic or lazy or dishonest. We should avoid behaviors that the proverbs say are characteristic of the fool, the sluggard, and the wicked. That's obvious and it's important. It's what we could refer to as the default teaching of this proverbial statement.

But as important as that teaching is and as obvious as it is—that we must not destroy our name and our reputation by reckless living—it is not the primary idea of this proverb. The sage isn't teaching us how to *not* have a *bad* name. He's not limiting his advice to helping us avoid ruining our reputation. The point of the proverb is cultivating a *good* name. Solomon's concern is that we invest our effort to cultivate an *esteemed* reputation. As important as it is to avoid a bad name and a negative reputation, *this* proverb goes beyond that and promotes the value of a *good* name. *That* is what's more desirable than great wealth. Solomon is saying that we should go for esteem, for a sterling reputation. *That* is what is greater than silver and gold.

In my first job, I had to hire 120 college students every summer. To help pick the ones I would hire, I required two reference letters for each applicant. Believe me, I read a *lot* of reference letters in those three years. I could sort them into three categories. There were those that said, "If you hire this moron you deserve to go out of business." Those letters referred to people whose names and reputations we just talked about. Those folks had a bad name and a terrible reputation.

A second category of letters is what this proverb is actually warning us against. I would get letters that essentially said, "This person is transparent. They are invisible. They don't do anything particularly bad, they just don't do anything particularly good or well. I hardly noticed them." These references were telling me, "This guy worked for me or he sat in my class, but I never saw anything that would make me remember him." Or "This girl ain't *bad*, she just ain't *good*." It's like the song they used to sing on *Hee Haw* about luck: "If it weren't for bad luck, I'd have no luck at all." These folks' reputation wasn't flawed, it just . . . wasn't!

Notice carefully what the proverb is saying. It isn't so much warning us against a bad name or a negative reputation. There are other proverbs that do teach that, but not this proverb. What this proverb is doing is praising and encouraging a *good* name and an *esteemed* reputation. There are a lot of "not bad" political leaders in our world. You could name a number of them quite easily. But the name Nelson Mandela stands out as a *good* name. We associate it with wise, compassionate, courageous leadership. It's a good name. There are hundreds of religious leaders in the world, but when we hear the name Mother Teresa we immediately associate it with a *sterling* reputation. Hers is a name that stands for compassion and sacrifice. It exemplifies what is good and right and noble. *Good* names! *Esteemed* reputations! *That's* what Solomon is calling for in this proverb.

Solomon is urging us not to settle for mediocrity. Don't go through life just trying to *not* fail. Athletic teams who play to *not lose* rarely win. I watched a TV special recently on John Wooden, the most successful men's college basketball coach in history. In this TV special they interviewed some of his former players who went on to star in the NBA. He had led each of them to NCAA national championships; they would forever have the distinction of being national champions. Coach's tutoring had prepared them for successful and lucrative careers in the NBA; they were millionaires many times over. But what these players most wanted to talk about was Coach Wooden's character, how he had taught them to be good men and decent human beings. Essentially, they reflected on how much they appreciated the fact that he taught them that a good name is more to be desired than great wealth and esteem as a person matters more than silver and gold.

On another occasion I heard Coach Wooden speak about his career as a coach, and he quoted a little verse I've never forgotten: "No written word, no spoken plea can teach our youth what they should be. Nor all the books on all the shelves—it's what the teachers are themselves." He knew that his best hope for developing people with good names, with character, with reputations worth having was to have one himself.

Do you see what this proverb is steering us toward? It is saying don't live a bad life, but don't stop at "not bad." It's about a *good* name. What really matters here is *esteem*. These are the writer's passions. Not everyone is going to have a famous name like Nelson Mandela or Mother Teresa or John Wooden. Those are the few among us. Solomon's not talking about celebrity, he's talking about significance. Maybe your name will never be in lights—or in print. Perhaps only a relative few will speak it, and according to this proverb that's okay. What Solomon wants us to understand is that whenever people do hear the sound that calls you to their mind, what they hear is a *good* name. Whenever that certain, specific sound is heard by the human ear—that sound that represents you—Solomon says that *great* wealth is less valuable than people associating that sound with a good name. The reputation associated with that sound *must* matter more to you than any amount of silver or gold you can dream of.

A second observation I want to make from this proverb is that the items Solomon chose to compare with a good name and an esteemed reputation don't come easily to us. Throughout this book of Proverbs, wealth and silver and gold are associated with the careful use of wisdom and knowledge and insight. Wealth and money are the product of hard, smart, disciplined labor. The fool and the sluggard don't obtain wealth; money goes to the wise and the industrious. A clear message in these proverbs is that if you want desired and treasured things, you have to work intentionally and wisely and industriously to have them. They go to those who work, and who work hard and smart.

So if that's true—and according to Proverbs it is true—is it not also true that if we want something that is more desirable and if we want something of greater value than these things, we must work for it as well? It stands to reason that a good name and an esteemed reputation are not treasures we fall into. There is no inheritance, there is no lottery or grand sweepstakes to win, there is no lucky slot machine in Vegas or in heaven that will drop a good name or an esteemed reputation in our lap.

Now, if I'm crazy enough to want a bad name, I should live like the fool or the sluggard or the wicked or the unfaithful, okay? And if I *don't* want a bad name I *don't* live like them. But this proverb isn't about a bad name. This proverb isn't even about a neutral name or a "not bad" reputation. This proverb *is* about a *good* name. This proverb *is* about *esteem*. So we wrestle again with the proverbial statement to figure out the answer to the questions "How can my name be good? How can my reputation be esteemed?" Before we go to the motivational literature for helpful anecdotes and illustrations, let's ask if Proverbs itself has any insight. And once again, Proverbs speaks loud and clear. Listen carefully to this wise advice from Proverbs 3, and consider how its teaching will contribute to your good name and to your good reputation. Let it serve as an answer to that crucial quest. I'm reading from Proverbs 3:1–10.

> My sons [and daughters], do not forget my teaching, but let your
>   heart keep my commandments;
> For length of days and years of life and peace they will add to you.
> Do not let kindness and truth leave you; bind them around your
>   neck, write them on the tablet of your heart.
> **So you will find favor and [so you will find] good repute in the sight
>   of God and man.**
> Trust in the Lord with all your heart and do not lean on your own
>   understanding.
> In all your ways acknowledge him, and he will make your paths
>   straight.
> Do not be wise in your own eyes; fear the Lord and turn away from
>   evil.

It will be healing to your body and refreshment to your bones.
Honor the Lord from your wealth and from the first of all your
produce;
And so your barns will be filled with plenty and your vats will overflow with new wine. (author's translation)

Sounds. Noises. Physiologically, mechanically that's all your name is. A sound. A noise. But that sound will generate an image in those who hear it. It will stand for wisdom, righteousness, honesty, integrity, trust, godliness . . . or not. As you leave here and go to make your mark on the world and the fortune that mark will earn for you, go with Solomon's counsel:

A good name is more desirable than great riches;
to be esteemed is better than silver or gold.

Commentary

When you think of an expository message what comes to your mind? Is it something pedantic and dull? Something filled with explanation? Or do you think of it as something light and humorous? Sid Buzzell uses an expository approach to Proverbs 22:1. It's for an after-dinner talk at Colorado Christian University for graduating seniors and their families.

In his introduction, Buzzell deals with sounds and noises. It takes a while before he gets down to what he's talking about. I think this is a great sermon for the audience to which he preaches. No one has a Bible. No one particularly wants to hear a dull exposition of some biblical point, so here is an exposition of a single verse that moves the audience to laughter and thought.

Interview

How long does it take you to prepare a sermon?

It varies. It depends on if it's a passage I've worked with before. When I was pastoring, I would go away for a week whenever I was beginning or thinking about a new series. I would do all the exegetical work and just bury myself. A man in our church had a cabin, and I went there with a bunch of books and worked through the passage and got the big idea of the whole book. I did all of the exegetical spadework and broke it down into sermons. I'd ask, "How am I going to preach this series?" Usually a maximum series length would be eight weeks. And when I came home, all of the exegetical work was done.

It would be hard to say how much time I spend on a sermon, because each week it would be another eight to ten hours for putting the actual sermon together. But I had already done that spadework.

Do you collect and file illustrations?

I do keep them. I tear them out of newspapers, but I find living illustrations work better. What works for me is talking to people. But I do collect them and I have a file on my computer.

How long was this sermon?

It was about twenty minutes or so. They wanted me to keep it under twenty-five minutes.

Do you preach with or without notes?

Most of the time with no notes.

What was the context for this sermon? Were there any challenges in terms of your audience?

It was an after-dinner speech, so everybody was full and ready for a nap. It was a banquet held the night before graduation for seniors and their families . . . Grandma, Grandpa, Uncle Fred, and all the people who come to graduation. We'd had all of these awards, and so by the time I got up there people were tired.

How did you come up with that passage for this audience?

I had this thing ruminating around in my head. I thought that it was something these kids needed to hear: You'll have lots of opportunities to sell out. In the short run you'll make a few bucks and in the long run you'll ruin yourself.

What do you need to know about Hebrew poetry in order to preach it well?

In Hebrew poetry, the lines work together. And my model when I'm working with a proverb or psalm is that the meaning is in the middle. The meaning isn't in the first line and the meaning isn't in the second line. When you rub the two lines together you get a spark, and that's where the meaning is. If you try to get the meaning from what's written there you spoil the proverb. That's the same with parables. You've got to ask, "What's the point here?" not just "Do you understand the first line, do you understand the second line?" You have to ask how the two lines work together because that's what the sage is saying. Truth discovered is more memorable than truth preached.

You also said that much of your sermon hung on the second functional question. Why is that question important in this particular sermon?

The proverb doesn't need much explanation. It's pretty clear what he's saying: A good name is better than gold, and a good reputation is better than great wealth. And that's nice church language, but it's stupid street language. You've got to be kidding me! You've got to be joking! Look at the world! I don't believe that. And in that kind of proverb the mystery is in the second part, not the first part. So with this group of people who just graduated from college and are going out to make their fortune, of course a proverb like this is far more characterized by what we don't say than what we do say. You could go on all night. The idea is that if you spoil your reputation, you spoil the opportunity to make the money. The best path—and I put that there in the end—the surest path to great wealth is a great reputation.

And any preacher worth his or her salt understands that you have to keep raising the question. Once doesn't do it.

What are the challenges in preaching a proverb?

One is you have to create more material, and the more freedom I have, the more I am apt to get in trouble. In Proverbs you're free-flowing, and so the danger is that I've got the proverb out there—a good name is better than gold, a good reputation is better than silver—and that's all he's told me. I have to make up the rest of that message. In a book like James you've got more explanation and context. In Proverbs I really don't have any other immediate material to work with.

But where else do I go? The first question I have to ask is "Where else does the Bible talk about this?" I don't want people to leave saying, "I got the point and thirty minutes of Buzzell's wisdom, which is really no better than mine. He's no smarter than I am. I got the point out of the Bible." We hear that Sunday after Sunday . . . a springboard off the passage. It's easy to make Proverbs a springboard for your own thoughts because you don't have that surrounding context. That's why I went to all of Proverbs to support the point. It's not true because I said it's true. It's true because here in the Bible God makes further explanation.

Yes, sometimes the passage is used as a springboard for the preacher's own thought.

I get two minutes of God and twenty-eight minutes of you.

What advice would you give to a young preacher, and what encouragement would you give to a seasoned preacher?

First, get a preaching calendar and figure out where you're going so you have time for both exegesis and incubation. If you don't let this idea form in your mind and in your heart, and if you get into the practice of Saturday night specials, you'll never be a decent preacher. Stay ahead of it. I don't know where I came up with the idea of going away six months ahead of time and doing all of that exegetical spadework. I would just lock myself away for a week and delve into that book and into that series and do the work. Fortunately I had a board who would let me do that. I worked twelve to thirteen hours a day immersing myself in that passage, and then when I came back, if I had to preach the next week's sermon two hours after I preached this week's sermon, I could do it because I knew what the passage was about. I knew the outline of it, the logic of it. I knew how this passage fit into the big sweep of the whole book. To go piece by piece, passage by passage without seeing how it fits into the bigger picture of what the writer is doing with the whole book is total nonsense. If you're going to do great preaching it takes time for that to form in your heart and mind. So that would be my advice to a young preacher. Stay ahead of it.

To a more seasoned preacher my advice is to avoid going stale. It's awfully easy to become so familiar with the Scriptures that we're no longer excited about God's Word. I have another saying I use in homiletics class: "It takes a real gift to bore people with something as exciting as the Bible, but we've got a lot of gifted preachers out there."

What are the questions people are asking about life? Preach those questions as a way to keep your audience alive. Howard Hendricks used to say, "If you listen to some preachers, you're highly qualified to live the Christian life in first-century Corinth, but you don't have a clue how to live the Christian life in the twenty-first century."

The key to the whole thing is getting ourselves impassioned about the idea of the passage and developing it according to the logic of the passage. When I hear pastors say they can't preach without notes because they forget the outline, I say they're not following the logic of the passage.

6

Ego Adjustment

Ecclesiastes 3:9–15

SCOTT WENIG

Exegetical Idea: After surveying the nature of life, Solomon concludes that by himself man is at a loss because God is the center of reality as the Creator, Provider, and (sovereign) Ruler over all.

Vision of God: Sovereign and good (redemptive and generous)

Point of Depravity: Frustration over our limitations or lack of control; temptation to take things for granted; failure to align ourselves with God's will and work

Point of Need: Put God at the center of life and operate from there.

Functional Questions: Explain and apply

Structure: Deductive

Homiletical Idea/Preaching Idea: God is at the center of reality and he is good.

Scott Wenig is the Haddon W. Robinson Chair of Biblical Preaching and professor of applied theology at Denver Seminary. He also serves as the director of the Denver Seminary Preaching Initiative and has more than twenty-five years of pastoral ministry experience.

He has contributed to *The Dictionary of Christianity in America,* the *Leadership Handbook for Ministry, Leadership Journal, Sixteenth Century Journal, The Journal of Anglican and Episcopal History, Preaching Journal,* and *Preaching Today,* and he is the author of *Straightening the Altars,* a study of the English Reformation.

Introduction

Back in the 1960s the mayor of Chicago was Richard Daley. He was famous for a number of things, most notably for being the last of the big-time bosses of the city. Daley was sharp, powerful, and had an absolutely enormous ego.

One time a speechwriter who worked for Daley came to him and asked for a raise. Daley was amazed that anyone would have the gall to do that. He told the guy, "I'm not giving you a raise. It should be enough for you that you get to work for me, a great American hero."

Well, a few months later it's November, and Daley is giving a speech on Veteran's Day. He was famous for never reading his speeches through ahead of time; he just enjoyed winging it in the moment.

So he's going on and thundering on about how valuable our veterans are and how forgotten they are, and he says, "But I haven't forgotten about you. In fact, today I'm proposing a seventeen-point program at the federal, state, and local levels, for us to care for our veterans." Now there's nation-wide press coverage, hundreds of people watching, and everyone is really eager to hear what Daley is going to say about this. And Daley himself is curious, so he turns the page in his speech.

And all it says is, "You're on your own now, you great American hero."

Transition (Curve—go slow)

We live in a society that exalts the ego; in our culture being number one is all too often what life is focused on.

We see that in sports, we see it in the world of entertainment, sometimes we see it in business, and I can personally vouch for the fact that we even see it in education.

But is that a good way to live?

Transition (Curve—go slow)

As many—if not most—of you know, that portion of the Bible we call the New Testament was written in Greek. The word translated "I" in Greek is a little word spelled E-G-O. Does anyone want to guess what word we get from that Greek word? Yes, it's *ego* . . . the center of who I am.

The ego is like anything else in our lives and our world: it can be something good, healthy, and godly, or it can become tainted, soiled, and sinful.

Because of our fallen condition, all too often our egos can get to the point where we think we're the center of the universe and we begin to act like we're in charge of everything and everyone.

Illustration: Management consultant Ken Blanchard says that sometimes ego is an acronym for "Edging God Out."

Have you ever done that? Have you ever let your desires, your will, your ego get to the point where you regularly say, "It has to be done my way because I'm always right"? Have you ever "edged God out" of your life, or at least moved him to the margins? I would guess that we all have on occasion, and when we do that, the results usually aren't very attractive or promising.

Illustration: John Calvin wrote, "For as the surest source of destruction to men is to obey themselves, so the only haven of safety is to have no other will, no other wisdom, than to follow the Lord wherever He leads. Let this, then, be the first step, to abandon ourselves and devote the whole energy of our minds to the service of God" (*Institutes of the Christian Religion* [Beveridge], 3.7.1).

Transition (Curve—go slow)

Solomon discovered the truth of what Calvin wrote. Throughout much of his life he gave in to his ego and put himself at the center of life only to discover that much of what he did and accomplished was fleeting—it was like chasing after the wind.

And here, near the middle of chapter 3 in his great book Ecclesiastes, he picks up on that theme. Look at verse 9: "What do workers gain from their toil?"

This verse is something of a rhetorical question, and the implied answer is, "Not really very much." Our honest reaction to that might be, "Hey, wait a minute; that's not necessarily true. I built a business, we raised a family, I got an education, and we built this fabulous new facility. What do you mean we don't get very much from our toil?"

To answer that, we have to look at this verse in the context of chapter 2. You remember that Solomon had looked at all the things he had experienced and accomplished—engaging in intellectual pursuits, giving himself to the pursuit of pleasure, acquiring and building a vast empire and a beautiful city, constructing a temple for God that was the envy of many ancient cultures. He discovered that it was all "vanity" or "fleeting," the key word that occurs thirty-eight times in this book. And you may remember that he concluded in 2:17, "So I hated life, because the work that is done under the sun was grievous to me. All of it is meaningless [fleeting], a chasing after the wind."

He got so frustrated because he realized that all the experiences he had, all the knowledge he gained, all the things he constructed were fleeting because he had put himself at the center of life. Those achievements weren't necessarily bad, and I would argue that from a human standpoint many of them were tremendous—let's give credit where credit is due—but they wouldn't last or endure.

Transition (Curve—go slow)

So at this point in his book, Solomon makes a really good decision. He turns his attention away from himself to the source and center of all reality, almighty God. Look at verses 10–11:

> I have seen the burden God has laid on the human race. He has made everything beautiful in its time. He has also set eternity in the human heart; yet no one can fathom what God has done from beginning to end.

Please note that God is the subject of these verses and that he is the one who is taking action here. He lays a burden on humanity (we'll come back to that). He makes everything beautiful. A better translation of that word from the original text is "appropriate." He sets eternity in our hearts. He is the One who works from beginning to end. Solomon is saying that God is the center of reality because he's the Creator.

Illustration: The Apostles' Creed is our earliest systematic articulation of orthodox Christian doctrine. Some of you may have grown up reciting this. It begins by saying, "I believe in God the Father Almighty, Maker of Heaven and earth." He's the Creator who made everything on our planet, everything in our solar system, everything in our galaxy—in fact, everything in our universe. And in what is certainly an understatement—something I'm not generally prone to do—we can say the universe is pretty doggone big.

Go surfboarding through our galaxy, the Milky Way, at the speed of light, which is 186,000 miles a second (Warp 1 on *Star Trek*). After 40,000 years you'd only be halfway across. Our galaxy is only one of millions of galaxies, and God made them all.

> "To whom will you compare me? Or who is my equal?" says the Holy One. Lift your eyes and look to the heavens: Who created all these? He who brings out the starry host one by one, and calls them each by name. (Isa. 40:25–26)

Like Solomon, Isaiah argues that our God is the Creator and he's at the center of reality. And as our text goes on to say, "He has put eternity in our hearts." This is a fascinating statement. It means we intuitively know that this earth and what we can see, hear, taste, touch, and smell is not all there is to life and reality.

But as the rest of that verse says, there's a catch. On our own we cannot figure out what God has done—or oftentimes what God is doing—from the beginning to the end, because we are limited.

Application: Friends, if you've been in the church world for any time at all, you've heard the saying "We're not in control." I know we say that a lot, but I think it bears repeating. Because in spite of all our education, knowledge, science, and technology (much of it is really, truly amazing), we still don't understand the way life works much of the time. It's a mystery and will remain so because we are limited.

Illustration: The death of Robb Williford. (Robb died from a severe strain of the flu just before Christmas in 2010.) Robb's son Tyler saw his mom Tricia emailing and said, "Please email daddy and tell him to come home." There is no explanation for an event like that, other than we're fallen creatures in a fallen world who sometimes unexpectedly get sick and die.

Some of you here this morning have experienced similar types of situations, and you may be wrestling with those today. I have bad news for you, but I also have good news for you.

The bad news is that our limitations and lack of control make life mysterious. As hard as we try, we're never going to figure it out. That's the burden God has laid on us that Solomon speaks of in verse 10, and in all honesty, that can be frustrating. But the good news is that God will make everything beautiful or appropriate in its time. This is part of the gospel!

Ecclesiastes 3:11 prefigures that wonderful section in the eighth chapter of Paul's fabulous Letter to the Romans where he writes, "And we know that in all things God works for the good of those who love him, who have been called according to his purpose" (Rom. 8:28). That verse can be and has been misused to the detriment of many suffering people, and I don't want to be guilty of that today. But I do want us to know that our Creator, who has made himself personally visible in Jesus of Nazareth, is so *good* that in his time he can turn even the most difficult and mysterious things in our lives into something appropriate, positive, and maybe even beautiful.

Application: So, friends, can I ask you a question this morning? Do you trust your God? I'm going to assume since you've expended the energy and taken the time to be here this morning that you believe in him, but do you trust him when life gets dicey and pain comes your way?

Please know that I'm preaching to myself here this morning. At points I've had some big losses, and I know from personal experience that it's not always easy to trust God in the midst of mysterious events.

Transition (Curve—go slow)

But this text tells us that our God is at the center of reality and that he can be trusted—even in the midst of mystery. It also goes on to tell us that we can trust him because he's our Provider. Look at verses 12 and 13:

> I know that there is nothing better for [people] than to be happy and to do good while they live. That everyone may eat and drink, and find satisfaction in all their toil—this is the gift of God.

Here we're given a powerful exhortation to engage life and enjoy it because all the good things we encounter come from the hand of God. Your family, your job, your health, your home, your car, your pets, this church—they're all gifts from the hand of the One who provides for us! Oh friends, this is *grace*—it's grace—our good God's lavish generosity poured out on his fallen and undeserving creatures!

Illustration: When I come home at night Melanie will greet me with her arms up in the air waiting for a hug. Our little dog, Darcy, always barks a greeting. Our bigger dog, Zach (he's a dog who knows the Lord), comes over and leans into me as a sign of love. I try to keep a picture of that scene in my mind and burn it into my memory because it's the grace of God in my life.

Friends, Solomon says to take the gracious gifts that our God so richly provides and enjoy them all and share them—whether it's eating, drinking, or engaging in our work.

Illustration: Quote from Tommy Nelson:

> Everyone is going to die. As you read this book, the clock is ticking. The 24-hour virus is waiting on you. There are germs in your teeth that will cause cavities. One day you'll have a root canal. All of those things are bad and they are coming.
>
> So today, while everything is OK, go get a double dip Rocky Road ice cream (or whatever flavor you love). Take some friends or family with you, lick your ice cream slowly, and just enjoy being together. Call an old friend you haven't spoken to in a while and get caught up. Rent a movie you've wanted to see and curl up on the sofa with some hot popcorn. Enjoy today—love God, enjoy life and have fun. (*A Life Well-Lived*, p. 53)

Solomon is telling us the exact same thing. He says, "Be as happy as you can, enjoy all the good parts of life, and find satisfaction in all that you do because *God has provided it all for you*."

Illustration: I've read a lot of history in my life, and I can tell you that we live in a time and place that Solomon in all his glory could not have conceived of. From indoor plumbing and heating to flying halfway around the world in a day, to iPods, iPhones, and iPads—it's all the provision of our good and gracious God.

Application: Our good and gracious God has provided so much for us, not least our salvation in Jesus. And our call is to respond to him with gratitude.

Illustration: In early 1939 the quiet first baseman of the New York Yankees, Lou Gehrig, discovered that he was dying of a horrible, debilitating disease. On the Fourth of July that year, he stood on the field of Yankee Stadium and thanked everyone who made his playing days with that team so wonderful. He thanked the fans, the groundskeepers, the vendors, the ticket-takers, his manager, his teammates, his parents, and especially his wife. He thanked everyone who made his job possible, and then he concluded his remarks by saying, "I'm the luckiest man alive." I can hardly imagine the character of a man who could express such gratitude while facing a horrible death, but I do know that in a culture where players hold out for millions more because they think they deserve it, the great ones always play with gratitude.

Are we thankful for the many good gifts God has provided?

Are we grateful that he's the center of reality and the source of our salvation?

Transition (Curve—go slow)

Solomon has shown us that God is our creator and our provider. But he's saved the most interesting part for last. Look what he says in verses 14–15:

> I know that everything God does will endure forever; nothing can be added to it and nothing taken from it. God does it so that people will fear him. Whatever is has already been, and what will be has been before; and God will call the past to account.

Let's note Solomon's description of God here: What he does will endure forever; he does all this so men will revere him; and he will hold us accountable. The point here is that God is the sovereign ruler of the universe.

The idea of a sovereign ruler over all is hard for Americans because we've never had a monarchy. Since 1776 we've never served a king or queen or a pharaoh or a string of dictators like they have in Egypt. We're a country that is a democratic republic, and our culture is pretty egalitarian by nature. We vote people in, we pressure others out, and we don't like it when someone gets too powerful or too rich or too big for their britches.

There are a lot of benefits to a culture like ours, but sometimes it hinders how we view God and his call on our lives. Solomon says here that God is the King and that he is the One who is in complete control. There's nothing and no one beyond his eye or his ear or his arm. And when he chooses to act, nothing or no one can get in his way.

Illustration: Lee Trevino appearing on *The Tonight Show*:

Johnny: "What'd you learn from getting hit by lightning on the golf course?"

Trevino shot back: "I learned that when the Almighty wants to play through—you let him!"

God is at the center of reality and he runs the universe, and as the text says, we're to *revere* him. But what does that mean? What does that look like?

Solomon is saying, "Don't fight God. Respect him. Make sure to put him at the center and align your life with what he wants." This text says don't let your ego get so big that it goes against the rhythm of creation.

Don't be selfish and take God's wonderful gift of sex outside of your marriage.
Don't take the good gift of food and turn it into gluttony.
Don't turn the good gift of drink and let it descend into drunkenness.
Don't turn your humor into coarse joking.

Since we're going to be held accountable, we need to make sure that what's on our hearts is in *alignment* with what's on God's heart. His heart is revealed throughout the Scriptures but especially in the life of Jesus. His heart is always to reach out to the least, the last, and the lost.

Illustration: Melanie and I at the Newseum. Great time—sports video, newspapers, Berlin Wall exhibit, 9/11 exhibit, then we went to the bottom floor on the far right side at the back for the Pulitzer Prize exhibit. Some of those pictures are fun or funny or exciting, but a lot of them are just tragic. One of them just wrecked us both. [Show the picture] Little Sudanese girl dying of hunger and Kevin Carter won a Pulitzer Prize but killed himself out of guilt.

Melanie was crying and I had tears in my eyes, and I said, "Honey, this is why Jesus has called us to feed the poor." And when we got home we adopted another child through Compassion International. We can't save 'em all but we can help save one.

Friend, if you know Jesus, you have gifts and time, talents and treasures. As his follower you're called to *align* your life with his rule and leverage some of your resources to extend his reign.

See, you don't want to live for yourself. You don't want to let your ego get to the point where you think you're at the center of life and that reality revolves around you. Solomon tried that and he found out that it only leads to a dead end.

Instead, you want to remember that God is good and that he's at the center of reality and then focus your life on him.

Conclusion

Louis XIV was the king of France in the last part of the seventeenth century and the early part of the eighteenth century. He called himself the Sun King, claimed that he was the nation of France, and overall had an ego that would put most politicians to shame. But like all humanity, he eventually died. His funeral was held in the Cathedral of Notre Dame in the evening, and it was lit by hundreds of burning candles in order to create an atmosphere of reverence for Louis.

Massillon, the archbishop of the cathedral, was assigned to preach the funeral sermon and he entered from a side door. Then he slowly walked in front of the king's casket and ascended to the pulpit.

It was completely silent and every eye was upon him. What would he say about the great king? How would he describe him and his many accomplishments?

Massillon waited a moment, eyed the congregation, then said, "Only God is great! Only God is great!"

He was absolutely right.

And you and I will serve ourselves, our families and friends, and our world well if we always keep in mind that our good God is the center of reality and he alone is great.

Commentary

Ecclesiastes is one of the most difficult books of the Bible to interpret. The ancient rabbis were hesitant to even put it in the Scriptures. The book itself seldom gets preached because of its difficulties. Scott Wenig is courageous enough to tackle this book. It begins with an interesting introduction, but along the way he takes time to make transitions. Unlike other preachers, he has directions in his manuscript that say "curve" or "go slow." In other words, he realizes that when he gets to difficult sections of the sermon he'll have to change his vocal pattern; in doing that, he can make the connections from one point to another.

Interview

How long does it take to prepare a sermon?

If it's a passage that I've never really worked on before, a fresh passage, it's probably going to take me somewhere between fourteen and twenty hours from working with the text all the way to finalizing the manuscript. If it's a passage that I have some familiarity with—if I've taught or maybe even preached on it before—but I'm reworking a sermon or doing something pretty fresh with it, I'm guessing it would take me twelve to fifteen hours.

How do you go about preparing to preach?

In terms of preparation, it depends upon the context of the sermon. When I was pastoring, we would go through books of the Bible and I would sit down and think, "Okay, here's the next passage I want to preach." I'd start with the text and then work through the exegetical idea and how to translate that into my preaching idea. Once I got that, then I sat down and thought through what I call—what Haddon calls—the functional questions, which I find enormously helpful. What in this text or in this idea needs to be explained, proved, and applied? Once I get the preaching idea, I'm thinking of the audience at that point. In terms of this text and this idea, what questions are the audience going to have? What are they not going to understand about this passage that I have to explain? What questions of doubt or uncertainty are they going to have that I need to prove? I'm big on application, so what difference does this make? I think every sermon in one way or another has to be applied, so I'm always looking for places to do what I call "press the pause button and apply."

So you don't save application for the end of your sermon?

You don't need to save the application until the end. You can apply as you go.

Do you use a preaching calendar?

When I was pastoring I always did.

Where do you find your illustrations? There's great variety in this one sermon.

Newspapers or books, journals, things I see on TV, movies. I'm pretty convinced in the current climate that experiences are probably the best illustrations.

Tell me about your manuscript. It's detailed. At the top of the manuscript you spell out exegetical idea, vision of God, point of depravity, functional questions. Do you do that every time you preach?

It keeps everything right out in front of me in terms of what the text is about and what I'm going to try to accomplish in the sermon.

Tell me about your use of transitions. You make those very clear in your manuscript.

Andy Stanley, in his book *Communicating for a Change*, talks about going into the curve, which are transitions. So I've adopted his language and I say, "Now I'm going into the curve." I need to slow down because I need to make sure that when I'm going from this movement to the next movement I don't lose listeners as I go through the curve. I think a lot of times when we're preaching we just assume that people are with us. We know where we're going, but the fact of the matter is that communication is not just what's said, it's also what's heard. And I think Andy's right: When you go into the curve, you've got to slow down. That means really developing and taking the time to focus on transitions, and taking your time as you preach.

What are the challenges in preaching Ecclesiastes?

You can pick up ten commentaries on Ecclesiastes and get twenty different interpretations of what the book is about in general. Simple questions like who wrote it and what's he trying to do are not easily answered.

The second big issue is that it reflects a different genre.

The third thing is not to get lost in the questions. Different sections of the book will apply to different people in different ways.

Can you suggest any books that might help us out?

First, Craig Bartholomew's commentary on Ecclesiastes is brilliant. Second, Philip Ryken published a book and preached a series of sermons on Ecclesiastes. Sidney Greidanus wrote an excellent book, *Preaching Christ from Ecclesiastes*. And a fourth book I'd highly recommend is a commentary on Ecclesiastes by Derek Kidner.

What advice or encouragement would you give to a young preacher or a more seasoned preacher?

Be yourself. Pray hard. Preach the Bible clearly. Those three things.

7

Overhearing a Counseling Session

Isaiah 43:1–3a

RAMONA SPILMAN

D o you ever feel that life is not fair? Class is canceled, but the assignment is still due?
Have you ever wondered where following the rules has gotten you? You asked God for help, but you weren't perfectly satisfied with the consequences. Accepted a job, moved your whole family, then got laid off? Been told you're too old . . . or too young? Waited up late for someone to come home and he or she never does? Jokingly answer the phone expecting a friend's voice, only to have the person on the other end identify herself as a representative of a hospital?

Have you ever been the wrong gender, wrong race, wrong faith? Have you ever asked how a loving God could let 9/11 happen? Or Columbine . . . cancer . . . acne . . . abuse?

I want to tell you a story along those lines, but as they say in the movies, the names have been changed to protect the innocent. These events happened a long time ago in a place far away, but the story is true.

It was one of those times when you know there is a problem as soon as you see the person. A woman I barely knew stood crying at my office door. Charlotte (I've changed her name) and I had worked together for over five years at that point. In some ways you might have thought we would be close. We were both Christians in an industry that was not exactly known

Ramona Spilman serves as pastor of adult education at Cherry Hills Community Church in Highlands Ranch, Colorado, where she teaches a weekly Sunday school class of two hundred women. Ramona also teaches preaching at Denver Seminary in an adjunct capacity. Prior to entering ministry, she worked as a purchasing agent in the maritime industry.

for falling at the feet of Jesus, although God's name was evoked routinely in heated conversations. But other than our faith, we had very little in common. We came from different backgrounds. We probably would have gotten along socially, but the occasion never arose, and our jobs often put us at odds. This visit, however, did not appear to be motivated by a business problem. I got her a cup of coffee and shut the door.

She never touched the coffee, but she did begin to talk. It seems that the day before she'd had a visit from child welfare. They came to remove her daughter from her home. Allegedly, her husband, the child's father, had been having sexual relations with their child. Charlotte knew it was a mistake, a horrible mistake. The problem was—it turned out to be true. Oh, and the story got worse. It turned out that her friends at church, the women she would normally have turned to, had known about the situation but had been afraid to tell her. They did not want to upset her . . . hoped it would just stop. They did go to the pastor; he fortunately called child welfare, but he didn't know how to deal with Charlotte. He was hoping to avoid any embarrassment to the church, and he did not contact her himself. Charlotte cried and cried, "What am I going to do? My daughter, the kids, I don't know who to turn to, even the church. How could God . . . ? I'm so alone, so afraid."

What do you say to a person who has been betrayed? When everything she depended on—her husband, her friends, and the church—has deserted her?

What would you have said to Charlotte? For that matter, what would you say to someone else if faced with that situation? What's been said to you? I wanted to say everything would be all right, but that would have been a lie. I thought a bit about abuse statistics, and I thought about telling her she was not alone—but that would not be helpful. For once I avoided platitudes. What would you have said? How do you process a situation when everything you value seems to be collapsing into devastation, out of control, and you feel isolated and alone? The worst thing probably would be quoting Romans 8:28 and promising that "God works all things for the good of those who love him." But what do you say?

The words of Isaiah 43 kept going through my mind. I did not bring them up with Charlotte; right then she just needed a friend, someone to make phone calls, walk beside her, hold her hand. Later we did talk about it.

We're going to look at it now. So if you turn with me to Isaiah 43, let's hear the Word of our God.

But now, thus says the LORD, your Creator, O Jacob, and He who
   formed you, O Israel,
"Do not fear, for I have redeemed you;
I have called you by name; you are Mine!
When you pass through the waters, I will be with you;
And through the rivers, they will not overflow you.
When you walk through the fire you will not be scorched,
Nor will the flame burn you.
For I am the LORD your God,
The Holy One of Israel, your Savior." (Isa. 43:1–3 NASB)

Powerful words. They sound good. The temptation is to leave it as just
words: to give lip service to a powerful God while believing that those
powerful words don't apply to you; to deny their truth in the face of reality,
a world falling apart while you are left alone in the wreckage.

The problem is that we like everything nice and neat. We're twenty-
first-century Americans who expect a guaranteed formula for everything
from success to salvation. We've taken God's promise that everything will
work out for good to mean that if you are a Christian you can "have it your
way." But that's not real life. That's not what God promised his people
Israel, and that's not what God promised Charlotte, and it's not what he
promises you, his people today. It's certainly not what he promises those
who will minister in his name.

God knows us pretty well. He could have just said, "I'm with you. I'm
God. Take my word for it, I'll be there." But he knows the human mind-
set. God or not, our question is always, "So what good does that do me
now? Why should I believe that God will be there for me amidst transition,
betrayal, in-laws, jobs, terrorist threats, sickness?" He doesn't ignore our
cries, he addresses them. He explains himself and invites us to consider
the implications. He starts by directing us to *remember*.

In Isaiah 43, God reminds us where we came from.

The backdrop of the text is telling. He is addressing Israel, the people of
God, and they were not feeling secure at all. Isaiah's words are addressed
to a people whose homes and cities had been devastated by enemies. They
went to temple (church), said their prayers, celebrated religious holidays.
They weren't perfect, but they sure were better than heathens—those other
guys. Yet they had lost their money and, in some cases, their families; they
were being forced to live and work just to survive. They did not like where

they were being forced to live. And all the pride they had in what they did, who they were, and what they had accomplished had disintegrated into despair. They may have lived three thousand years ago, but they were just like us when we feel taken advantage of or deceived. They, like my friend Charlotte, could scarcely believe they had been so foolish. They had been so gullible to think this kind of thing could never happen to them. They never saw disaster coming. Oh yes, they should have, but those they thought would protect them had let them down. Their hopes and expectations were smashed. But despite what looked to be overwhelming odds stacked against them, God said, "Remember, I created you and I formed you. Remember where you came from."

New beginnings—the birth of a child, passing an exam, sometimes just making rent—those are the things that give us hope. The Bible tells us that God created the world out of nothing. Impressive. And just as amazing, God created us. The psalmist tells us that God formed the bones in this hand [raise hand], intricately weaving the body parts to work together. God saw and knew you before you drew your first breath. Some of us may have questions about his design, but the psalmist insists God intentionally created us—you and me—as individuals. *Remember*, God says in the midst of your struggle. *Remember*, I created you, formed you. You are not an accident. *Remember*, I am not surprised at where you are at right now. *Remember* where you come from, *remember* who you are. I am your God. You are not alone. *Remember*.

God then says to not fear but instead be comforted in the fact that not only did he create and form you, me, all of us, but he has redeemed us as well. Remember, you, me . . . we're not alone. *Redeemed* is sort of a "churchy" word, but it's actually a contractual business term. If you've ever posted a bail bond for someone, you probably understand the concept to some extent. But it's more than that. God is reminding me, you, my friend Charlotte, that he paid a price for us. We cost him something. He gives us a picture of what that means, a story recorded in the fifteenth chapter of Genesis. You may know the backdrop of this passage. The book records that in the beginning God created the earth, but despite his kindness Adam and Eve decided to do things their own way . . . flat-out disobedience to God's commands (they obviously did not care what God wanted). The result (in church we call it "the fall") had disastrous consequences for all of us.

But even then God promised that evil would not win. He would see to that. The intimate relationship experienced by Adam and Eve before the fall was over, but God's promise indicated that it could be restored. The next six chapters record humankind's attempt to live life without God and the unfortunate results of denying his existence. But beginning with God's call to Abraham, the promise of Genesis 3 begins to be seen. Over the next couple of chapters God enters into a covenant with Abraham and promises him and his descendants a number of things. We could spend a great deal of time discussing the intricacies of this agreement, but in the interest of time, we will just look at how it informs God's promise of his presence in Isaiah 43.

Today, the word *covenant* has lost much of its meaning. It is unlikely that any of you has ever finalized a real estate contract or financial investment with this kind of blood oath. But in the ancient Near East the significance of this ceremony would have been self-evident—and shocking. Genesis 15 describes the preparation for the ceremony as follows, beginning in verse 9: "'Bring me a three year old heifer, and a three year old female goat, and a three year old ram, and a turtledove, and a young pigeon.' Then he brought all these to Him and cut them in two, and laid each half opposite the other; but he did not cut the birds" (Gen. 15:9–10 NASB).

Then in verses 17–18 the ceremony is recorded: "It came about when the sun had set, that it was very dark, and behold, there appeared a smoking oven and a flaming torch which passed between these pieces. On that day the LORD made a covenant with Abram." And the chapter concludes with a description of the land and its inhabitants.

The relationship between one in a power position (like God, called the *suzerain* or king) and one without power (like Abraham, called the *vassal*) would be established by a treaty. The vassal would make promises to the suzerain lord; for example, "I will be a friend to your friends, and an enemy to your enemies." Then a blood ritual would always conclude the treaty ceremony. Records indicate that just like in this passage, it involved an animal split in two and a bloody path walked between the parts: the one without power always walked the bloody pathway, symbolically saying, "May the same happen to me and more if I do not keep my promises to you, great king." History shows that the people of the ancient Near East took this promise literally.

Now imagine the impact of understanding what happens here in Genesis 15, when the almighty King, God himself, walks between the bloody animal parts, signifying his promise that he would keep his covenant with

Abraham and pay the cost should Abraham or his descendants fail to keep up the bargain. In this act God is saying, "May the same happen to me and more if this covenant is broken."

And broken it was, over and over again by those who professed to follow God. In the Gospel of John, the fulfillment of God's promise begins to be realized with the coming of God in Jesus Christ: "The Word became flesh and made his dwelling among us" (John 1:14 NASB). God said he alone would see that the covenant was fulfilled. He alone would pay the price. Isaiah describes the suffering Savior, the Lord of Glory who was to come. John merely says, "The word became flesh and dwelt among us." You know the rest of the story: Darkness fell at the cross as it also fell in Genesis 15. The sword's violence, the torn flesh, a blood-strewn pathway, death, abandonment. God's promise was a commitment that saw fulfillment in Jesus's walk to the cross. God's promise to Israel, to those who follow him today, says, "I have paid the price for sin, for the breaking of the covenant. I have redeemed you."

There's a lot of evil in this world. The newspapers, Charlotte, and I bet any number of you can testify to the fact that good does not always seem to come out ahead. You don't always see an immediate payoff for following Christ. We look back to that historical event of Christ on the cross. Because of this we belong to Christ, but at times that redeeming work seems so far away that it brings little comfort. Can God really know what we're going through? Sure he knows in the big sense of the word . . . but can he *know*? When we read that Christ redeems us, we understand that he saves us. But we also need to remember that in the process of helping us out, his friends deserted him, one denied knowing him, and he was betrayed by a kiss. Does God understand Charlotte's sense of betrayal and desertion? In one sense, wasn't she too betrayed by a kiss?

The way Christ died, as well as the fact that he did die, shows that God understands that life is not always pleasant. Since when has life ever been a good time had by all? Most of us here have passed at least one sleepless night asking God, "Why?" When plagued by doubts and filled with questions, our awareness and trust in God's goodness tend to evaporate. Even if you do trust, life is sometimes hard. Do you ever want to pray "Thy will be done" but are not really sure whether you mean it? God, through Isaiah 43, calls you and me to *remember* . . . you are not alone. God has redeemed you. You, me, we belong to him.

God says, "Remember." He created us, formed us, and redeemed us, and then he gets really personal: "Remember . . . I have called you by name." God knows your name. You, me, we are not anonymous. You can get away with being anonymous many places, even in church if you want to, but before God there are no secret identities. He knows us, me, you . . . for better or worse, God knows you personally.

I grew up in a small town. I haven't lived there in over twenty-five years, but to this day, when I go back home and visit the local bank or grocery store, someone will inevitably stop me and ask if I'm a Spilman. In their mind they know whom I belong to and where I come from. They know my name. They know my folks. They can tell stories and know more history than I care for them to know. But because of that, there's connection. They know where I come from and whom I belong to. They know my name.

The use of one's name implies relationship. Otherwise it's just, "Hey, you." When God calls us by name, he says, "Remember, my servant Ramona"—or fill in your name—"remember that [insert name] may appear to struggle with early onset Alzheimer's. She needs a name tag, but I don't. I, the living God, have not forgotten you; you are not alone. We're in this together. I, the Lord your God, call you by name."

If the passage ended here, the promise of faith would sound good but be terribly unrealistic. No one would buy it. But the Bible is realistic and it makes some things very clear. If you identify yourself with God, if you are called by his name, and even if you are redeemed, you will very likely experience tough times. The oft-heard accusation that Christianity is somehow divorced from life and exists merely as a sedative is absurd.

To use Isaiah's words: "*When* [emphasis is important here] you pass through the water and through the river, and *when* you walk through fire . . . remember, God will be there." The key word here is *when*. There will be water and there will be fire, and Isaiah's not talking about a campfire on a beach in this passage. Fire and water show up as symbols of danger, trials, and judgment throughout the Old Testament. Trials and troubles in life will happen.

We live in a real world, and consequently we will suffer, sometimes horribly. Unexpected accidents, sickness, death are all to be understood as part of our existence. People will disappoint us, hurt us, and sometimes even betray us. Broken relationships, lost jobs, major embarrassing moments, and even incest may have to be faced by God's people. So God says, . . . "Remember."

Remember who you are, whom you belong to, who will never let go of you—*when* the fire burns and the water takes your breath away. When insecurities take over and inadequacy overwhelms. When, as Paul points out in his Letter to the Corinthians, we are afflicted, we will not be crushed, persecuted but not forsaken, struck down but not destroyed. And remember—you, me, my friend Charlotte—we are not alone.

The hope we find in Isaiah's words does not offer a grin-and-bear-it kind of psychobabble or a theology based on positive thinking. It's not just psyching yourself up to meet the problem at hand. My friend Charlotte could not have just "put on a happy face" and expected all to be well. Her daughter was hurt, Charlotte was devastated, and her family would never again be the same. Well-meaning Christians had contributed to the problem; there were no easy solutions. She was not interested in false reassurances of the good life that comes along with faith. But she was not alone.

God's Word offers us an eyes-wide-open, realistic approach to life's situations. When you go through the waters (and you will) and when you are overwhelmed by the waves of emotion and fear (it's a guarantee), do not panic, do not give up. Remember, God promises to be with you. When you go through the fire and all seems out of control (and it may be by any reasonable human evaluation), and when you have no place to turn, remember the Lord your God knows who you are and wants to walk with you through all that goes on in your life. God created you, formed you, redeemed you, and called you by name. God is not surprised by your situation; you do not have to go through this alone. God promises to be there. Call upon his name.

And don't forget the bottom line: If we let you down—and we probably will at some point—our God won't. Remember who God is. He is the Holy One, your Creator. He designed the beating of your heart, the veins that run through to your toes. He is your Redeemer who knows the desolation of intimate betrayal, who was not only *willing* to die but *did* die in order that you might live—truly live—not just survive. And he knows and calls you by name. God knew Charlotte's pain, and he knows yours and mine. The presence of God is the hope we have to offer each other and a world that appears to consider injustice normal.

Charlotte had lots of details to take care of and tears to cry, but she was not alone. And you, me . . . we're not either. When you walk through the fire and when you are overwhelmed by the flood, remember: Jesus the Christ, the living God, the Holy One of Israel is your Savior. He knows you and calls you by name. You are not alone. Remember.

Commentary

Ramona Spilman gave this sermon at a theological seminary and also at a church. In a sense, she isn't preaching to an audience at all. She answers to a woman by the name of Charlotte. Charlotte's story is the story to which this preacher speaks. Like any story, it has a need. It gets us to listen. She says that she avoided platitudes talking to Charlotte and asks the questions, "What would you have said? How do you process this situation?" It's Charlotte's problem primarily that she addresses with the sermon from Isaiah 43.

A lesson to be learned from this sermon is that sometimes a message is stronger if not spoken directly to the audience but to a character introduced to them earlier in the message. Overheard communication often has great power.

Interview

How long does it take you to prepare a sermon?

Ten to fifteen hours a week.

Tell me about your sermon preparation process. How do you go about preparing a sermon? Do you use commentaries? If so, how early or late in the process?

I use commentaries early on. I read through the passage. I still look at my Greek and Hebrew. I look to see if there's anything that stands out as a huge issue. I start with a more critical commentary, otherwise it's really easy for me just to slide into application without making sure if what I'm applying is correct.

Do you write an outline?

I do more of a flow. I do a formal outline at some point. I do a lot of teaching and then I do some preaching. My preparation for both is identical. I manuscript everything.

I write a manuscript, but I don't use it up front because I can't read when I'm up front. I use yellow sticky notes in my Bible. I manuscript so I know what I'll want to say.

Tell me about this particular sermon. How did it come about? Did you start with the passage or the situation with Charlotte or something else entirely?

I was invited to speak at Denver Seminary, and Isaiah 43 captivated me. I was also trying to think about a real-life situation that's not very churchy. I hesitated to use her story with this passage because it's extremely messy.

So not every need fits every audience? Your need is specific to your audience?

I'm very specific. If I were to preach that sermon here at Cherry Hills, I could use that illustration. I might not flesh it out as much as I did there. I would probably add more humor. There's a lot of humor about the irony of an accountant and a purchasing agent even working together in the shipping industry.

It's a pretty serious message, but comforting too.

To me, the power of the gospel lies in the fact that God does meet us in the messiness. He doesn't necessarily take away the messiness, but he is still God through it. I used to believe that for God to be God, everything had to be happy. But I wouldn't believe in that God now, because that's not real.

What did you do before going into ministry?

I worked in the maritime industry as a purchasing agent. I was in charge of materials management for a shipping company out of Houston, Texas. I was in the maritime industry for years, so I don't have a wealth of older stuff to draw from because I wasn't doing it then.

What were the challenges in preaching this particular passage?

Anytime you introduce something of a sexual nature from the pulpit, especially something like incest, you have to realize that some form of sexual abuse is a huge problem in our population. That's true in our congregation of 3,000 to 4,000 people on a Sunday. Some of them would be involved in this. I was conscious when I preached this at seminary that these people are going to be in ministry and they had to face the reality of what's going on in the culture. I wanted to be real because I wanted people who are preparing for ministry to know what's going on out there.

Is there any particular advice you'd give to a female preacher?

If an audience can't see your eyes, it bugs them. It sounds silly, but it is true. The hair can be a problem for women. I don't want it to matter, but it does.

Use a variety of illustrations that apply to your congregation—male, female, young, old.

Remember you are female, so don't try to be a guy. Don't try to be what you're not. Don't let gender become an issue. If they don't like you because you're female, that's okay. But if they don't like you because you gave a crummy sermon, that's not okay. You can't do anything about one, but you can do something about the other. You don't want gender to be an excuse for anything.

How do you end a sermon? Do you typically end by praying?

In our church we end with prayer. The worship team comes up to the platform during that time. I try to tie the prayer to the sermon, and if I know there is a song following, I always try to tie it to that as well. I always begin with prayer, too. It calms me. I always try to connect it to the last worship song or two and to what I'm going to say. The prayer is specific to what's happening that Sunday.

So the flow of the entire service is important?

Usually that's the case. I'm not big into the idea that "there has to be a flow," but I like there to be a tie. We should be walking this thing together, and what we've proclaimed in song is just a continuation in prayer.

Do you utilize media and technology?

I will do different things depending on the sermon. Sometimes I won't use anything, but nowadays that's rare. We've gotten so visual as a society. I'll use quotes, Scripture, or pictures on the screen if it applies to something I'm doing. I routinely use props, and we have cameras that focus in on the props so people can see them. That's important when you have 2,500 people in one service.

I probably use props more than anything else. They can go anywhere with you. I'm not real gimmicky, so when I have a prop, it's *a* prop and it symbolizes something. In one particular sermon on community, I built a Jenga tower. When I talked about the tendency to disconnect from community, I removed pieces until the tower finally collapsed.

8

Training the Mouth
of a Preacher's Kid

Jeremiah 1

KENT EDWARDS

Now, at least according to my program, I am supposed to preach. It's a strange thing, preaching, isn't it? I mean, Christian ministers do that all over the world. You have Christian ministers standing behind pulpits such as this every week—sometimes two, three, four, six, and more times a week—to preach God's Word. But it's a strange thing when you think about it, about the fact that these are real people preaching to a real world. A world filled with sin. A world that has been twisted by iniquity. I mean, how in the world do they think that preachers—that their words, the little puffs of air that they speak, puffs of air that are here one minute and gone the next—are going to make any difference, any impact, on a world that has been so affected by sin?

After all, if you pick up the *Times* and look at the front page, you will see that this world has been drastically, horribly affected by sin. You will see that there are wars and rumors of wars; that there are injustices, evils; that there are drug dealers who are growing rich over the bodies of middle-class kids; that there is the world of abortion on demand; that children are being slaughtered on the altar of convenience and preference; that there

Kent Edwards is professor of preaching and leadership at Talbot School of Theology/Biola University. He is the founding pastor of Oasis Community Church in Yorba Linda, California, and president of CrossTalk Global. He has more than twenty years of pastoral experience, both as a senior pastor and as a church planter. In addition to ministering regularly at churches throughout the country, Dr. Edwards is a popular conference and seminar speaker and lectures internationally in academic settings. Dr. Edwards previously served on the faculty of Gordon-Conwell Theological Seminary. He has published numerous articles and papers in the area of homiletics and is the author of *Effective First-Person Biblical Preaching* and *Deep Preaching: Creating Sermons That Go Beyond the Superficial.*

is adultery; that there is murder. We live in a society and a world that has been profoundly affected by sin. And Christian ministers who stand to preach, as you may do when you find yourself behind a pulpit—you will soon find yourself looking out over a congregation of real people who are facing real, desperate needs. You will see a person sitting in the corner who is suffering from an addiction. It could be alcohol, it could be sexual, but they are suffering from an addiction. You will know of a person in your congregation who is suffering serious legal charges. You will know of couples in your church whose marriages are being torn asunder. You will stand and you will look at those people, and you will say to yourself, "What in the world can I offer them? How can I straighten these twisted lives? How can I address the significant sin issues by offering these little puffs of air? What good is that going to do?"

When you find yourself asking those questions, I think it's safe to say that at least in one point of his life Jeremiah would have agreed with you. When we come to the text of Jeremiah we come to look at the life of a realist. In chapter 1 we read that Jeremiah was one of the priests of Anathoth. He was a preacher's kid. His dad was a priest. He spoke God's Word. I know that he lived during the reign of King Josiah of Judah, and Josiah rediscovered the Word of God. And there was a brief time in Judah's history where a light began to dawn and hope began to surface because perhaps this was a king who would practice righteousness.

But you know that Josiah came and began to minister in a world that had already been deeply infected by his predecessors. Manasseh had been king. Manasseh had given himself to evil. He had, with the power of legislation, brought idolatry into the land. And not just into the land; he brought it right into the temple itself. He had deliberately and willfully infected the people of God with sin. And it had taken root, not just in his life but in the next king to follow.

I think that as a preacher's kid Jeremiah would have overheard conversations similar to what preachers' kids overhear today. Then as now, I'm sure preachers got together to swap war stories, to tell each other how bad things were. They would talk about the latest terrible happenings that were going on in the world and the futility of the religious leaders to address them. These were priests outside Jerusalem, and inside Jerusalem there was idolatry going on in the temple. They would be talking about those things, and I think Jeremiah, as with any preacher's kid, probably would have been around the corner listening. Hearing the stories. Aware that the church was infected. Wondering if there was any good anyone could do in a situation that bad.

So on the day that the word of the Lord came to Jeremiah saying, "Before I formed you in the womb I knew you, before you were born I set you apart: I appointed you as a prophet to the nations" (1:5), I don't think that hit Jeremiah as particularly good news. I think he was saying to himself, "For crying out loud, God, I appreciate the fact that you have custom made me to serve you, but why didn't you give me a task where I could make a real difference in the world? Why not make me a doctor or a lawyer or a politician or a baker? Or anything? Why a preacher? What am I going to do with little puffs of air?" I think you get a glimpse of that in Jeremiah's response when he says, in essence, "O Sovereign Lord, I don't know how to speak. I am only a child. I don't have the experience. I don't have the training. I don't have the wherewithal to take my puffs of air and arrange them in a way and speak them with a force that will untangle the sin in the lives around me."

I don't think his heart was necessarily encouraged when we read here in verse 10, "See, today I appoint you over nations and kingdoms to uproot and tear down, to destroy and overthrow, to build and to plant." I mean, look at the scope of that ministry. God says, "I am calling you to be actively involved in this world." There are six different verbs, four of them destructive. Four of them. To uproot and tear down, to destroy and overthrow—words that are used elsewhere in Scripture to talk about a marauding army and the devastation that it would cause to opposition.

God says, "I am calling you to lay waste to the strongholds of sin. I am calling you to do battle with the bastions of the evil one. I am calling you to destroy the inroads that Satan and his evil ones have made in the hearts of the people and the nations as a whole. And when that's done, I have more for you. I have two more verbs for you. I want you to build and to plant. I want you to nurture and grow and develop people; to cause growth and healing."

How in the world is a man supposed to do that with little puffs of air? Why a preacher? How in the world is a preacher supposed to accomplish this kind of a task? I think it's absolutely impossible—unless you're given help. Unless you're given a tool to accomplish that impossible task. Notice what that is.

"You must go," God says in verse 7. "You must go to everyone I send you to and say whatever I command you." And then Jeremiah records in verse 9,

"Then the LORD reached out his hand and touched my mouth and said to me, 'I have put my words in your mouth.'" In one of the most poignant descriptions of the preaching task, God says, "You don't understand the task that I am asking you to do. I am not asking you to speak *your* words to the people. I am taking *my* words and I am placing them in your mouth." Your job, the job of the preacher, is not to speak your own words but to speak God's words. That's what makes the difference.

Barclay—that's William, not Charles—William Barclay says in his book *New Testament Words* (p. 185), "In Jewish thought a word was more than a sound expressing a meaning, a word actually did things. The word of God is not simply a sound, it is an effective cause." That's the word that Jeremiah is given. A word that is different than my word, a word that is different than your word. A word that is different than any parent's word. A word that's effective.

There are times in the morning when you say words as a parent: "Get up." "Have breakfast." "Do your homework." Sometimes those words result in absolutely nothing (or so I have heard from other parents). There is no positive effect. They are there, they fill the air, but they don't result in changed behavior in any way, shape, or form.

But God's words are not like our words. God's words are impregnated with God's power. So when God speaks, things happen. When God speaks results must come, they have to come. Which is why Isaiah can say that God's word will never return to him void but will always accomplish the purposes that he has sent forward (see Isa. 55:11). Always. Because it's not the power of the preacher, it's the power of God.

Look with me at chapter 1 in the book of Genesis. You see it so clearly there: "In the beginning God created the heavens and the earth." We read in verse 3, "And God said, 'Let there be light,' and there was light." Think about that for a minute—with the power of just his word, God created the biggest bang the universe has ever experienced. Suddenly, worlds and stars appeared out of nothing just because of the power of his spoken word. You read a little bit later on where he said, "'Let the water under the sky be gathered to one place, and let dry ground appear.' And it was so" (Gen. 1:9). And it happened. And it was so. That easy. That effortless. I mean, think of the geological plates shifting and moving, the tectonic forces that would be at play. Think of the volcanoes. Think of the mountains being formed as these plates hit each other, the enormous forces that are going on here, and it was all accomplished just by God saying, "Let it be." That's the power of God's word.

You see the power of God's word in the New Testament when Christ spoke. He sees the paralytic and says, "Take up your mat and walk"—and he does. Even surgeons today could not do that. He takes the spinal cord and fuses it together. He regenerates what we cannot regenerate with the power of just his word.

Jairus comes to Jesus. He says, "My little girl is dead." Jesus comes and says, *"Talitha koum!"* which means "Little girl, I say to you, get up!" (Mark 5:41). With the power of just his word life floods into her body. Her eyes are opened, and the first thing she wants is a milkshake. She can't wait to eat. That's life, supernatural life that comes because God's power has been infused through his word.

When God asks us to speak, he doesn't ask us to speak *our* words; he asks us to speak *his* words. And when we speak his words, our words have a supernatural power and authority that they never could have otherwise. We don't speak on our authority and our power, we speak with God's authority and God's power. All God's preachers have known that.

Moses knew that. He was a failed leader on the backside of nowhere when God came and said to him, "Go to Pharaoh the god-king and tell him that I have said, 'Let my people go.'" And it worked. Moses goes into the courtroom of the most powerful man in the world and says, "Let my people go"—and Pharaoh does. He has to. How could he stand against that kind of power?

Nathan the prophet comes to David and speaks the word of God to him in the situation involving Bathsheba. He says, "You are the man," and David repents and changes. A life is transformed. Sin is broken. Healing and growth occur because God's word is spoken.

Jonah goes to Nineveh. In obedience he delivers God's word, "In forty days you will be destroyed." Not the most winsome sermon I have ever heard, but it was God's word. And the nation repented. The destiny of the nation changed because God's word was spoken.

Every preacher who has made a difference has understood that God's word is powerful and he has harnessed God's word. Think of Luther in his little cell, his little room. He discovers the book of Romans, understands what God is saying, and has the courage and the audacity to say that to the world. Even though he himself may not feel adequate, God's word proves adequate. And the history of the church, the history of the entire world, is altered because of that.

I think of John Wesley, a man who spent his life on horseback going from place to place and preaching because he was convinced that God's word is powerful, that God's word is able to change lives, that when he spoke God's words he could tear down and he could build up. When he preached people responded, and a nation was transformed. Historians look at England and they look at France, so close and enduring the same basic socioeconomic principles and forces. They wonder why France went through the terrible revolution and why England was spared, and they will say it was largely because of one man, a preacher who spoke God's words.

We have seen that here too. In this area we have experienced that. Jonathan Edwards lived at a time when America had seen better days. The country was formed on religious principles but had drifted from them. J. Edwin Orr tells us that during the time when Jonathan Edwards lived in New England there was terrible moral decay. There were more children born out of wedlock than in wedlock. Gambling had gotten hold of a great number of people. Alcoholism had run rampant, even among the clergy. Many ministers were still so drunk on Sunday morning that they couldn't find their way to church to preach. But one man, Jonathan Edwards, believed in God's word. He believed in its inherent power, and he preached a sermon. Maybe you've heard of it: "Sinners in the Hands of an Angry God." As he read his manuscript—and I am told his delivery was, frankly, unimpressive—God's word went forth and gripped the hearts of people, and they cried out to be saved. The strongholds of Satan were defeated, new life began to develop, and the Great Awakening took place. The history of the church was changed and the history of the nation was changed because a preacher decided to speak God's words. And the world began to experience the power of God.

Of course God gives a requirement, a condition on this. He says to Jeremiah as he gives him this assignment, "You must go to everyone I send you and say whatever I command you. Be careful when you preach that you preach my word but only my word. Be careful that you do not take liberties. Be careful that you do not go further, that you do not say things other than what I have said."

If you read the book of Jeremiah, you will see that he is anxious, that he is angry at the false prophets who pervert God's word and take liberties with it and hurt God's people because of that. God says, "I have called you to say what I have told you to say. Your job is to faithfully communicate my word." He even gives Jeremiah a test right here in the text. Did you notice that in verse 11? "The word of the LORD came to me: 'What do you see, Jeremiah?' 'I see the branch of an almond tree,' I replied. The LORD said to me, 'You have seen correctly, for I am watching to see that my word is fulfilled.'" God gives Jeremiah a vision. Then he says, "Now tell me what you have seen. Can you accurately report what you have seen? Are you going to add to it? Are you going to embellish it? Are you going to change it? Are you going to modify it? Or are you going to faithfully communicate it?" When he says it accurately, God says, "Well done. You get an A in exegesis."

God does this again with a vision of a boiling pot, and then he says in verse 17, "Get yourself ready! Stand up and say to them whatever I command you." We live in a day in which we are not sure of the place of the preacher, but the Bible is sure of the place of the preacher. The Bible says that our place is to transform the world, to break down the strongholds of sin, and to bring healing and renewal with the power of God's Word. We do that by being faithful to it.

The job of the faculty is to help you, so when you end up preparing to preach you will be able to take the natural unit of Scripture, crack it open, and see the idea that God originally intended to communicate. When you break it open and see what's inside, it's like splitting an atom. You unleash enormous power, nuclear power, power you can harness to transform people's lives, to transform your church, to transform the world. The place of the preacher is to transform the world through faithful preaching of God's Word, and it works.

Nine years ago, my wife and I had a change in assignment. We left a church we were pastoring in Edmonton, Alberta—a church that was large, a church that was growing, a church that was healthy. We left to plant a church in Toronto. You need to know that Toronto is not overwhelmingly Christian. Toronto is very postmodern, very resistant. But I didn't want to end my life having always built on someone else's foundation. Like the apostle Paul, I wanted to plant a church. It felt very romantic while we were still in Edmonton.

We packed up the car and began driving toward Toronto, pulling the U-Haul behind. As we were going across the prairies, I suddenly realized the decision I had made. I was scared to death. I pulled the car over to the side of the highway and said to myself, "What in the world am I doing? I've never had a course in church planting. I didn't get an A in it. I'm going to a couple of people living in a hotbed of postmodernism; white-collar baby boomers with too much education, too much money, too much debt, and too much on their schedules. I'm supposed to plant a church in the midst of this? The list of people who have failed is a mile long. How in the world is this ever going to work?"

But I was convinced what God says to Jeremiah is true, that when God gives us his words we have his power and his authority. So with great fear we kept driving. Last Easter the church we started and the daughter church that we started had almost a thousand people worshiping God. At those moments you stand back and say, "I could never have done that, but God's word can. And God's word will."

The place of the preacher is to transform a sin-sick world by faithfully preaching God's Word. God called Jeremiah. God calls us.

Commentary

Notice the introduction that Edwards uses for his sermon. He imagines he's up on a platform and according to his program he is supposed to preach. He describes preaching as puffs of air and then he asks, "What can I offer them? How can I straighten out these twisted lives? How can I address these significant sin issues by offering these puffs of air. What good is that going to do?"

Have you ever wondered about the futility of preaching? Edwards is assuming that preachers have all thought about that question. He doesn't fully develop/state his idea until the end. The place of the preacher is to transform a sin-sick world by faithfully preaching God's word. So the sermon is inductive, but along the way the preacher works to keep the audience with him. As you read the sermon, assess whether you think he has succeeded or failed.

Interview

Tell us about your sermon preparation process.

The first step is to get into the biblical text and figure out the big idea. What in the world is going on here? I think in broad strokes. My objective is to ask, "What was the need in the ancient world that this passage is meeting? What itch is this going to scratch? What is the problem and what is the solution for it?" My goal is to understand not only intellectually but emotionally. I need to know the broader context, and I haven't understood it until I have felt it.

How do you *feel* a passage?

I have to feel the angst of the situation in the ancient world. I have to realize why this was a serious problem and why the solution was helpful. I understand it was a serious problem when it makes sense to me today. The Bible was written to a specific situation, but it was written for more than a specific situation. God wants to communicate to all people the lesson that was learned in this specific situation. I want to know the specific situation in order to feel the angst that they felt until it resonates in my own life.

Sometimes the Bible talks about a pain that I haven't been consciously aware of, so it surfaces a need I didn't know I had.

Tell me about your introduction. What are you trying to accomplish?

One of the things I want to do is identify with my audience. I want them to see me as one of them. There's a barrier because I'm standing up and they're sitting down. I want to make that disappear in their mind's eye. I want to crawl into their life and tap into their frustrations. One of the things I'll do is be really honest in my introduction. I want to describe what life is really like.

I want to speak to the audience's natural angst. This is narrative. I need to say that our struggle is the protagonist's struggle in the biblical narrative. I need the audience to say, "I am like Jeremiah." In a million ways we are different, but in this passage I think there's a tremendous resonance between the life of the honest preacher and the life of Jeremiah. He was frustrated too. I'm trying to have my listeners see there is a similarity, a link, a connection between their ministry situation and frustration and Jeremiah's.

The nice thing about a narrative is that narratives are concrete theology rather than abstract theology. We see theology in action. The extent to which the audience identifies with the protagonist is the extent to which this sermon will touch their lives. I have to keep saying, "You are like Jeremiah" so that when I give the big idea at the end, they have felt the frustration.

How do you deal with historical background information? How do you know what to say and what not to say?

I liken it to when I get my taxes done. My question to my accountant is "How much do I owe?" She knows all about tax law, but I don't want to know that. I want the bottom line. When she tells me what I owe and I say, "What?!" she will give me enough of her technical background for me to say, "Now I understand and I'm willing to write the check."

You only have to give the information that relates to what you're preaching, and you only give enough of that to make people say, "Now I'll write the check."

How would you define expository preaching?

Any preaching that exposes the listener to the big idea of the biblical text is expository. The audience has to see that it came from the Bible.

What's your opinion of preaching and the use of media?

I don't want outlines up on the screen, because if you use an outline it's usually an excuse for being unclear. If people don't know what I'm saying when I'm saying it, then I'm not being clear. God chose to communicate through the incarnation, so I think communicating incarnationally is one of the most powerful ways to preach.

I'm not against the use of media, but it's really hard to use it well. Can you think of a single movie that everyone in your church has seen? A metaphor is more common; for example, if I use a metaphor involving a coffeepot, everyone knows what that is. If, however, I'm speaking to a group where I know technology will communicate better to them, then I'll use it.

You don't use notes when you preach. Why?

I wouldn't buy a car from a salesperson who couldn't look me in the eye and tell me why this car is worth my money. I couldn't convince my wife to marry me if I had to read my proposal off a sheet. Whatever someone loves—fly-fishing, stamp collecting—he can talk to you about it off the top of his head. If you have meditated on something, spent time doing what I call the "closet work," it becomes part of you. If I can't remember it without notes, my audience will never remember it without notes. If they need an outline to remember it, they won't be carrying that outline to work with them on Monday morning. They need to carry it in their heads.

What about illustrations? Where do you find them?

I get them from life. I have learned that if I find something interesting, then other people are probably going to find it interesting. When I find something interesting, I ask, "What is it that makes this interesting?"

If you are working in a text and you are meditating on it, you will have more images than you have time for. But I will say that I have never forgotten what Haddon told me years ago when I said to him, "You're so good at images. Can I buy a book of images?" He said, "If you do it, you'll do it."

I think in pictures now. If you can't come up with a metaphor to explain the big idea after you finish your exegetical work, then you don't understand the big idea. Proof that you understand the big idea is that you can give a great metaphor for it.

What advice do you have for a young preacher, and what encouragement do you have for a more seasoned preacher?

Do not be deceived by your gift. Gift alone will not give you the ministry that your heart longs for and God wants. Paul told Timothy that he had to fan into flame the gift he'd been given. God gives you the gift, but you need to develop it. That takes a lifetime of work. Evaluate yourself. Malcolm Gladwell, author of *The Tipping Point*, says it takes ten thousand hours of your best possible concentration.

For the seasoned person, don't think it's all about technique. Your best asset is the Holy Spirit. The same way that a college-bound kid would never take SATs without help from a tutor, we would be foolish not to consult the Holy Spirit when preaching. Ignoring the Spirit is how we can have technically perfect sermons that don't do anything.

Walking down into Carlsbad Caverns is absolutely breathtaking. It is staggeringly beautiful to see what has been developed below the surface. The Holy Spirit does that. He takes us down into the biblical text. He can give us insight into the heart of God and into ourselves. There's no end to the cultivation of our relationship with God, and preachers should be drawn deeper into the heart of God the deeper they go into ministry.

9

The Insanity of Stewardship

Daniel 4

Torrey Robinson

Purpose: To challenge people to give to God and to his work at First Baptist Church through "Find Us Faithful" (church stewardship campaign).

Idea: Our position and our possessions are given to us that we might use them to bring glory to God.

Stance: First-person sermon from Nebuchadnezzar's perspective. As God sent Daniel to explain Nebuchadnezzar's dream to Nebuchadnezzar, the Persian monarch now visits First Baptist Church to explain God's message on stewardship.

Have you ever thought about insanity? To tell you the truth, I don't believe too many people give it much thought. We shun the mentally deranged from our circles and lock them away someplace where they will not bother us. At least that's how we treated them in my day. I don't suspect that even 2,500 years have caused people's perspectives to change much regarding insanity. Being around such people makes us feel uncomfortable. We don't know how to deal with them.

Because we are uncomfortable with it, because we are more comfortable locking such people away, we don't really have to give insanity much

Torrey Robinson is senior pastor of First Baptist Church in Tarrytown, New York. He previously pastored churches in Wisconsin and New Jersey. He's the coauthor of *It's All in How You Tell It: Preaching First-Person Expository Messages*.

thought. There is a saying, "Out of sight, out of mind." In this case, I might say that those who are out of their minds are kept out of sight to be out of our minds.

But for a moment I would ask you to give some thought to being out of your mind. As I have thought about it, I have come to realize that being insane is usually quite—how do you call it?—rational. That is, most insane people are really rather rational. We think of those who we call crazy and lock away as believing round things to be square, black things to be white, up to be down, nonsense to make sense. But that is seldom the way it is. As I see it, I'm not sure anyone is truly insane, they are merely acting on presuppositions that are wrong.

Let me try to explain what I am saying. I knew a man who, for reasons no one knew, came to believe that the house in which he and his family were living was no longer there. I do not know what he saw when he looked at the ceilings or walls, but from time to time he concluded that his house was gone. At times he would wake up in the middle of the night and wander through the house, awakening his family, pulling them from their beds, telling them that they must leave because the house was gone. They concluded that he was quite irrational. I, however, believe he was quite rational. If you woke up to discover that your home had been destroyed or was missing for some other reason, you too would likely wake up the rest of your family to convey this distressing news. No doubt the man was quite insane, but he was also quite rational. He was merely acting on faulty presuppositions. His thought process was quite normal, but his view of life was quite warped. I submit to you that a man who believes he is a donkey is acting quite rationally if he chooses to live outside and eat grass. Still, we recognize such a man as insane because, in fact, he is not a donkey. The basis of his thinking is all wrong.

I tell you all of this because I speak as an authority, for I am a man who was cursed with two types of insanity. I cannot convey to you the anguish and pain this caused me. I have been sent to you this morning to tell you my story, in order that I might warn you so that you might learn from me.

I suppose I should begin my story by introducing myself. Sometimes I forget to do that because in my day I never had to introduce myself to anyone. You see, my name is Nebuchadnezzar. You can read my story in the Old Testament book of Daniel in your Bibles. I understand that most of you do not know me, some of you have never even heard my name.

But it would not be so in my time. I tell to you without boasting that in my day I was the most influential and powerful man in the world. I was Nebuchadnezzar, king of Babylon. I ruled most of the known world. What I decreed was law. Whatever I wanted was mine. When I spoke, everyone listened.

I not only conquered and ruled, I also built. Even if you have not heard of me, perhaps you have heard of Babylon, the capital city that I rebuilt after the fall of the Assyrian Empire. I constructed a chain of fortresses both north and south of the city. I built impressive temples, palaces, canals, and streets. One of the building accomplishments in which I took the most pride was the Hanging Gardens of Babylon. These were a series of gardens built in terraces to please my Median queen who missed her native mountains. I understand that the Greeks later considered the gardens to be one of the Seven Wonders of the World.

At the height of my power, influence, and success I was brought down. One night I was awakened in the middle of the night by a dream that deeply disturbed me. This dream was more than just a dream. I was sure it was a vision from the gods. In the dream I saw a great tree. Its height was enormous. The tree grew large and strong, and its top touched the sky. It was visible to the very ends of the earth. Its leaves were beautiful, its fruit abundant, and on it was food for all. Under it the beasts of the field found shelter, and the birds of the air lived in its branches; from it every creature was fed.

As I watched this vision, there appeared before me a messenger, a holy angel coming down from heaven. He called in a loud voice:

> Cut down the tree and trim off its branches; strip off its leaves and scatter its fruit. Let the animals flee from under it and the birds from its branches. But let the stump and its roots, bound with iron and bronze, remain in the ground, in the grass of the field.
>
> Let him be drenched with the dew of heaven, and let him live with the animals among the plants of the earth. Let his mind be changed from that of a man and let him be given the mind of an animal, till seven times pass by for him.
>
> The decision is announced by messengers, the holy ones declare the verdict, so that the living may know that the Most High is sovereign over all kingdoms on earth and gives them to anyone he wishes and sets over them the lowliest of people. (Dan. 4:14–17)

I was not sure what this vision meant, but I feared that it involved me and my kingdom. So I called the magicians, enchanters, astrologers, and diviners to ask that they explain my troubling dream, but they could not interpret it for me. Finally, I called Belteshazzar into my presence—that is what I called him. I believe you are most familiar with his Hebrew name, Daniel. Some years before he had interpreted another troubling dream for me, so I explained this terrifying vision to him.

At first Daniel looked perplexed. He seemed upset by what I had told him. I did not know if he was troubled for me or if he feared for his life for telling me news I did not want to hear, so I told him that he should not let the dream or its meaning alarm him.

He proceeded to explain the meaning of the dream to me. He told me that I, Nebuchadnezzar, was the great tree that I saw in my vision. That part of his interpretation I liked, but that was only part of my dream. Daniel went on to explain the meaning of the angel's message to me. He told me that I would be driven out to live with the wild animals, that I would eat grass like cattle and be drenched with the dew of heaven. He said that it would be seven years before I would acknowledge that Daniel's God is sovereign over the kingdoms of men and gives them to anyone he wishes. He concluded by telling me that I should accept his advice to renounce my sins by doing what is right and by being kind to the oppressed. Perhaps, he told me, my prosperity might continue.

I knew Daniel was sincere. I even believed that he had accurately interpreted my vision. But I was the most powerful man in the world. Vision or no vision, I simply would not believe that anyone could drive me from my throne, not even Daniel's God.

After hearing Daniel's interpretation, at first I found myself on edge, but I was at the pinnacle of my success. There were no threats outside or inside my empire, and after about a month or so I began to relax. It seemed foolish that I should have ever worried at all. But a year later, I discovered for myself the reality of what Daniel had predicted.

I was walking on the roof of the royal palace in Babylon, surveying the city and admiring all my magnificent accomplishments. I can still remember my words, for they were the last words that I uttered for seven years. In my pride I said to myself, so that everyone could hear, "Is not this the great Babylon I have built as the royal residence, by my mighty power and for the glory of my majesty?" (Dan. 4:30).

But no sooner had I, the king of Babylon, spoken than I heard the voice of one speaking for the King of heaven: "This is what is decreed for you, King Nebuchadnezzar: Your royal authority has been taken from you. You will be driven away from people and will live with the wild animals; you will eat grass like the ox. Seven times will pass by for you until you acknowledge that the Most High is sovereign over all kingdoms on earth and gives them to anyone he wishes" (4:31–32).

And it was as the King decreed it. Immediately I became convinced that I was a beast, a wild animal—I don't know . . . a donkey. I desired to live in the fields and to eat the grass. With time my hair grew long and my fingernails grew like the claws of a bird. For seven years my insanity left me isolated and alone. I was afraid of people, yet I longed for companionship. I thought of myself as an animal, and yet no animal would come near me. I, the great king of Babylon, had been reduced to a demented creature, an outcast in my own kingdom.

What I have been telling you about is the condition that those closest to me are most familiar with. I suppose you could call it my public insanity. As the angel had predicted in my vision, it lasted seven years. But there was another insanity that preceded my public insanity. In fact, this other insanity was essentially the cause of my public insanity. I suppose you could call this other condition my spiritual insanity. No one else really noticed it, except perhaps for Daniel and his God. I have since come to realize that most people are afflicted by this inner spiritual insanity. No one else seems to notice because they all share the same faulty presuppositions.

The reason I am here this morning is because I fear that some of you may be likewise afflicted with this same inner insanity. God sent me to warn you as he sent Daniel to warn me. But when Daniel warned me I refused to listen. He interpreted my vision, he told me that I would lose my sanity, but I was already spiritually senseless, and as a result I never listened to him. I pray that you will listen to my warning even though I refused to heed Daniel's warning.

What is this spiritual insanity about which I am warning you? What is this spiritual condition that perhaps has you in its grip without your even knowing it?

There is an inner insanity that is an insanity of pride. Because most of those around you have been likewise afflicted, no one else may ever see it in you or call it to your attention. It is a senseless pride that says what is mine is mine. For me it was reflected in those words that echoed in my brain for seven years: "Is not this the great Babylon I have built as the royal residence, by my mighty power and for the glory of my majesty?" This spiritual insanity is reflected in our sin, when we shake our fists in the face of God and say to him, "Leave me alone! I'm going to live my life the way I want to live it!" It may be reflected in your attitude, just as it was reflected in mine, an attitude of pride that says, "What is mine is mine."

Sanity, seeing things as they really are, recognizes that all we have—our positions and our possessions—is not ours to keep but ours to manage, to use for the glory of God.

If you are a business or professional person, think of how you are spending your life. If you are spending your time and energy to build a company or a position or a practice in order to become affluent, to grow in influence and prestige and personal comfort, there is nothing that I know to suggest the King of heaven is the least bit interested in your success. You are crazy to think that giving your life for those ends will have any lasting value.

On the other hand, if you are committed to the business or professional world in order to use the gifts God has given you to build his kingdom and bring glory to him, then you have invested in one of God's choicest projects. Your time and energy are being invested with eternal dividends. Your efforts will be directed toward functioning as a beachhead for righteousness wherever God has put you. I saw it in Daniel, shining in the pagan world of Babylon. As with him, personal profit will become unimportant. The glory of God, manifested in all you do and say and demonstrated in the sheer excellence and integrity of your work and witness, becomes your priority.

Or suppose you are working to provide yourself with a home, to the extent that you are giving of your life's energies to build a place of personal luxury—beautifully furnished, in the right neighborhood, designed to indulge your personal tastes, and, not incidentally, to impress those who may be watching. God's Word would seem to indicate that your efforts have no lasting value. There is an insanity to that. You are pouring your most precious possessions—your time, your energy, and your money—down the drain of prideful self-indulgence.

On the other hand, if you make decisions about what sort of house you need in light of God's purposes for a home, everything you invest there may be of eternal value. For instance, viewing your home as the prime place to model godly values to your children will mean that the choices you make will be geared to God's purposes. Treating the house as a center of Christian hospitality and as a launching pad for spreading God's good news in your neighborhood will dictate God-centered decisions. In this way the efforts you put into providing a genuinely Christian home wind up invested for eternity.

Let me suggest one other example. This insanity of pride shows itself on a morning like this. I understand that at the end of your worship today you will be asked to make financial commitments to God. As a king, I know that there is a way in which people can think of such a commitment as giving a tip to God. After all, he deserves it for being there when we need him. But whenever you give an offering or make a commitment to God, it should remind you that God doesn't exist for you. You exist for him. All that you have is his, entrusted to you to be used for his glory. It is not a question of how little you can give without embarrassing yourself, but of how much you can give to expand God's kingdom and bring him glory.

After seven years of living like an animal, I recognized an even greater insanity. I had been clinging to the faulty presupposition that what is mine is mine. Because I refused to recognize my error, God took everything away. You might say he made me insane so that I might truly understand the way things are. It was then that I raised my eyes toward heaven and my sanity was restored. Once I was cured of my spiritual insanity, the insanity of pride, God restored my mind.

> Then I praised the Most High; I honored and glorified him who lives forever. His dominion is an eternal dominion; his kingdom endures from genera-tion to generation. All the peoples of the earth are regarded as nothing. He does as he pleases with the powers of heaven and the peoples of the earth [even wayward kings]. No one can hold back his hand or say to him, "What have you done?"
>
> At the same time that my sanity was restored, my honor and splendor were returned to me for the glory of my kingdom. My advisers and nobles sought me out, and I was restored to my throne and became even greater than before. Now I, Nebuchadnezzar, praise and exalt and glorify the King of heaven, because everything he does is right and all his ways are just. And those who walk in pride he is able to humble. (Dan. 4:34–37)

Commentary

This is a first-person sermon and is based on a passage that is also a first-person testimony. Most first-person sermons are built on accounts that are not first-person passages. But it is possible to take a passage like this one about Nebuchadnezzar and turn it into "Three Things We Can Learn from Nebuchadnezzar." Some people question whether it is proper to take a passage written in the third person and turn it into a first-person personal testimony. I've never understood that objection because preachers can take a passage that is not first person and turn it into "points" that are not in the passage or fill it with illustrations that the passage does not suggest.

As you read Torrey Robinson's message it draws you in, and you'll find that it's a great way to communicate a difficult truth to people who may not want to hear it. The questions that Torrey answers after the sermon are the same questions other people would ask. Since he has written a book on the subject, he's a good person to look to for answers.

Interview

How did you come to choose Daniel 4 as a stewardship text?

Years ago I heard Gordon MacDonald talk about stewardship and he referred to Daniel 4. That's what got me thinking about that passage. I hadn't preached on it, and we had a stewardship program at our church. I thought it would be a fun thing to do. Gordon MacDonald's message wasn't from Daniel, but he referenced Daniel. I guess with every sermon you're standing on the shoulders of other people when you're exegeting or pulling files.

How do you decide when to preach a first-person sermon?

I have routinely done a first-person sermon sometime during the Advent season and at Easter. I do one for Easter because we have so many people who visit, and it seems like such a seeker-sensitive form. There are so many different slants that I can take as a first-person witness to the resurrection. It gives me different ways to tell the story.

More often than not, I'll come to a passage that I didn't originally think about doing as a first-person sermon. In this case I was thinking about doing a stewardship sermon and I remembered Gordon MacDonald referring to the concept of master/owner. As I read Daniel I thought, "This is a testimony; this is a first-person story." I have found that first-person sermons are actually fairly easy to put together when they come out of a text that has that flow to it.

What is the role of imagination in a first-person sermon?

It helps you do exegesis when you allow yourself to imagine. Your imagination has to be tied to the text, just like your interpretation is tied to the text. I thought of Nebuchadnezzar and his greatness and how easily he could have this perspective of "What's mine is mine." I wrote a whole book with my dad on first-person sermons. I don't know if I preach more of them, but I do a lot more narrative sermons, and imagination is important.

How do you choose your perspective?

The perspective has to do with which person I view the text from. In this case it's a first-person story, Nebuchadnezzar's story. It was Nebuchadnezzar who should tell the story because that's what happens in the text. But when I do a first-person sermon at Easter, I may tell the story as the soldier at the foot of the cross, who in the Gospel of Mark says, "Surely this is the Son of God." He's certainly not a major player in the story, but his comment is important and that would lead me to a fresh perspective on the story.

Sometimes a bit player gives a fresh perspective. I'm still guided by what the biblical writer is saying, but the different perspective gives it a freshness. It's usually one of those two things. Either the text itself really tells the story from one perspective, as it seemed to in this story from Daniel, or other times I'll try to take a fresh perspective.

Do you typically use one stance, or do you change it up?

I do typically use the same stance, but not always.

There are times when I bring people back in time from the twenty-first century AD to the first century BC. It's harder to do application that way because I'm mostly reenacting the story. I'm really not talking to these people, so if I bring the congregation back in time, almost invariably I will have them be part of the story so that as a character I am still talking to them. I'll have the audience imagine they are sitting there and that will allow me to talk to them more directly. That's why I have some technique or device to allow the character to speak directly to the audience.

When the audience goes back in time it's harder to talk to them about stuff in modern times, so I don't do that as often. More often I'll have the character step forward and tell his story to the modern audience. That allows me to assume that maybe I know a few things about them and it makes application a lot simpler.

Does it take more or less time to prepare a first-person sermon than a traditional sermon?

Most of the time, the actual sermon manuscript is not significantly different to that point. In this particular sermon the exegesis and writing were probably a little faster because I literally just took portions of the text and made them part of my manuscript since I'm telling Nebuchadnezzar's story. When I preach it, I don't usually try to memorize the verses, but some verses I felt it very necessary to memorize. I memorized the last few verses because of Nebuchadnezzar's great testimony of exalting and glorifying the King of heaven. I wanted to say that in the way it was recorded in Scripture. I feel there's a fair amount of flexibility for Nebuchadnezzar to tell his story with imprecise wording. Having said that, when I prepared the sermon I actually copied portions of the text and knew that I was going to reiterate that in some way in the sermon.

Where sermon preparation becomes longer—and where this sermon took longer—has to do with costuming. I did this in a costume, and thinking through the costume adds time. If somebody hasn't done a first-person sermon, then they're starting from scratch. I have several different costumes that can combine. I have a basic wardrobe. It doesn't take very long, but then I might put on a beard. I don't remember in this case whether I tried to dye my hair. . . . I've actually done that a time or two, but usually I'll just put some kind of a hood on. But costuming can add anywhere from an hour or two to several hours. It depends on how readily available the costume is and how elaborate it is. There are a number of first-person sermons I've done where I had no costume at all and prep time really ended up being the same as a regular sermon.

Would you use a prop if you're not in costume? Does the congregation need some kind of signal?

I think a prop helps. I've done something as simple as starting out with a coat and tie on and then just taking my coat off. It could be something really simple in order to differentiate.

How many hours would you say you need for sermon preparation?

I think most of the sermons I preach I put together in about sixteen to twenty hours.

And you preach without notes?

Yes. And I don't think you can preach a first-person sermon well with notes. I can't imagine someone telling their story by reading it. I think there's more power in doing it without notes. People obviously do get up front and share their testimony at our church, and if they're not comfortable speaking they bring notes. But even then they'd be better off without notes. From a communication standpoint and from an authenticity standpoint, it's better to tell your story than read it.

Do you write an outline and a manuscript?

I always have an outline, and 90 percent of the time I have a manuscript. If I could, I'd always have one. Occasionally I'll be so pressed for time that I'll have to shortchange it. But I definitely feel more comfortable and more prepared if I have a manuscript, even though I don't bring it up in the pulpit with me.

How does a manuscript help you?

It helps me to think through what lines I really want to work on. There are two or three lines in this sermon—and a couple were directly from Scripture—that I wanted to get right. I remember there's one line in there about what insanity is that I wanted to state a certain way. By manuscripting it, I can think through how to craft the wording better. It also helps me image the sermon better. I find myself thinking through it as I'm writing in a way that I wouldn't do as thoroughly if I didn't manuscript it.

Do you use a sermon calendar? How often do you plan to preach first-person sermons?

Ideally, I would say I put a sermon calendar together for the year. There are certain times of the year when I'll think about doing certain types of sermons. When it comes to first-person sermons, really it's probably Christmas and Easter and two or three more times as I'm exegeting a text. I'll think, "This will really make a good first-person sermon." I try to allow the text to lead me to the form rather than approach the text with a predetermined form.

Can you preach a first-person sermon too often?

Not if you let the text determine the form. A couple years ago I deliberately chose not to do a first-person message at Easter. Even though it has been my tradition, I found that I couldn't do it and feel that it was fresh. I think you have to be true both to the text and to what you feel like you can do well. The key is if you do it well, people won't even think in terms of the form. They'll just think, "That was a good sermon." In a first-person sermon, the form is unique enough that people may think about that. I've been in my church for over fifteen years and I've done them often enough that people don't find them as novel as they once did, but they know whether they really profited from the sermon or not.

What made you try a first-person sermon in the first place?

I started out when I was new in the ministry and I was insecure about my preaching. I found that doing a first-person sermon allowed me to hide as a character rather than stand up there in front of people. I felt safer as somebody else. Now that I've been preaching for thirty years I don't suffer from that same anxiety, but that got me started in a way that was beneficial. Now it's obviously easier just to be me.

Do you always write out your idea and purpose at the top of your manuscript?

I had the opportunity to teach preaching in an adjunct capacity in a few different places, and I stress that to every student. It helps me to be intentional about why I am preaching this sermon. We were having a stewardship campaign for this particular sermon, so the purpose was almost given to me. I always ask, "Why is this here in Scripture and why is this important for my congregation to hear?" It also makes me think in terms of the application.

What are the challenges in applying a first-person sermon?

Well, having read quite a bit of Fred Craddock, I think that one of the values of narrative preaching is that sometimes indirect communication can be more powerful than direct. When my audience thinks of the application for themselves, that can be more powerful than if I say, "This is what you have to do." I want to make sure they do have something they're going away with. There's always that tension, depending on my stance. This particular sermon I was able to approach from the standpoint of a king who had learned a lesson. I could just feel that if he had the opportunity to come back and tell others about this experience, he wouldn't be shy about telling people what they needed to do. What I don't want to do is preach at people when I'm telling a story. That's the difference between a narrative sermon and a traditional sermon. In a traditional sermon, I'm really up there to exhort and to directly challenge people; in a narrative sermon, whether it's a first-person or not, I'm not quite as direct.

In my experience, most pastors don't like to talk about money. Do you think a first-person sermon is a good way to bring up an unpopular subject?

The response I got was very positive, and this sermon was probably more direct than some first-person sermons might be. But I think the directness came out of the sense I had that Nebuchadnezzar would certainly want to impress upon people that this is very important. I wanted to stress the importance not because the church needs the money but because of their relationship to God. The entire service was unique and special, but it made the first-person sermon a fitting climax to it.

Why should a young preacher try a first-person sermon?

I think we just need to have more variety in our preaching. There shouldn't be one form that we use all the time. The Bible uses different forms. I think we need to choose forms that bring out the truth of Scripture effectively.

What about a more seasoned preacher?

My guess is that the preachers who struggle the most with first-person sermons are preachers who are really uncomfortable preaching without notes. I don't know that for a fact, but the students I get the most pushback from are students who are just scared about standing up without notes. I think it's easier to preach a first-person sermon without notes than a traditional sermon. The one caveat is that when I preach without notes in a traditional sermon, I have my Bible open and the Bible really becomes my notes. There are times when I've preached a first-person sermon where I don't have my Bible open because of the stance I'm taking. Stories tell themselves, so if people will dare to try preaching without notes, I think it's a great medium to try doing that. And I really think that if somebody does it well, the response of the congregation will get them to do another one.

10

Jonah's Shady Outlook from His Sunny Lookout

Jonah 1–4

Matthew Kim

Homiletical Idea: Christians care about what God cares about.

As we go through this sermon series on "Men of the Old Testament," today we're going to study a familiar Bible character who is often mentioned around the globe in children's Sunday school classes. For pastors, preaching on a familiar passage can be the kiss of death, as it was for poor Eutychus who in Acts 20 fell asleep during one of Paul's sermons and plummeted from a third-story windowsill. But please stay awake today in your seats, because God has a message for each of us to apply in our lives.

The prophet Jonah's story is legendary because a large, mysterious creature of the sea not only swallowed him up, but he even lived to tell about it. That's not something that many of us can boast about in *The Denver Post*. But on that peculiar day, his story may have found its way onto the front page of *The Assyrian Gazette*. Today we won't get bogged down by the slimy details of which aquatic species sampled Jonah. Instead, we're going to focus on the central message that this short book conveys,

Matthew Kim is an assistant professor of preaching and ministry at Gordon-Conwell Theological Seminary in Hamilton, Massachusetts. He previously served as senior pastor of Logos Central Chapel in Denver, Colorado. He is the author of *7 Lessons for New Pastors: Your First Year in Ministry* and *Preaching to Second Generation Korean Americans: Towards a Possible Selves Contextual Homiletic*. He has written numerous journal articles, book chapters, and book reviews, and his sermons have appeared in *Preaching Today Online, Preaching, The Preacher*, and *The College of Preachers Journal*.

which concerns an inner struggle for all of us. That battle within each of us concerns the condition of our hearts: Do we have the heart of Jonah or the heart of God?

To set the scene, God commands Jonah to go to the city of Nineveh in the country of Assyria to warn the Ninevites of their wickedness and rebellion. Nineveh was one of the most populated cities at this time with over 120,000 inhabitants. To put this into perspective, the average population of a city in the ancient world was about 30,000. The Assyrians were prideful and unspeakably cruel toward their enemies.

At first, Jonah doesn't go to Nineveh; he tries to flee from God and from his responsibility to preach to these people whom he despises. He travels westward with a group of sailors who are heading toward a city called Tarshish. God causes a great storm to hit the waters, and the frustrated sailors eventually throw Jonah off the boat. For them, Jonah's just taking up space and weighing down the ship. That's when he's swallowed by a large creature and remains inside of it for three days and three nights.

As Jonah sloshes around inside of the fish, he recites prayers from the book of Psalms. Eventually God causes the fish to spit Jonah out onto dry land. God gives Jonah a second chance to warn the Ninevites of their sin and their need for repentance. Having spent days in the fish's belly, Jonah finally comes to his senses and obeys God. So he preaches in 3:4, "Forty more days and Nineveh will be overthrown." Then, in verse 5 we read, "The Ninevites believed God. A fast was proclaimed, and all of them, from the greatest to the least, put on sackcloth [which was a very coarse fabric made from goat's hair]."

We have to understand that the people of Nineveh, even a short time ago, would never have repented. They were a stubborn, arrogant, cruel bunch who boasted in their mighty army. However, at this point the Assyrians had tasted a bitter piece of humble pie and were suffering due to famine and a waning military presence. Because of this instability, they were meek and more open to Jonah's prophetic challenge. So in verse 10 we read, "When God saw what they did and how they turned from their evil ways, he relented and did not bring on them the destruction he had threatened."

You might think, "Fantastic, this is a story with a happy ending!" The Ninevites confess their sins, God is merciful, and everyone is happy, right? Wrong! Let's continue to chapter 4, starting at verse 1, which states, "But to

Jonah this seemed very wrong, and he became angry." Jonah, the prophet of God, is extremely angry with God. Why? First, he's upset because God spares and forgives his enemies, the Ninevites. When you absolutely hate someone, you don't want them to experience any type of good fortune. Jonah's furious with God because God chooses not to destroy Nineveh as he had promised. In 4:3 Jonah cries out, "Now, LORD, take away my life, for it is better for me to die than to live."

What Jonah demonstrates here is a very human response, isn't it? Have you ever experienced Jonah's emotion? Has there ever been a time where something good happened to someone you didn't like? How did you feel?

When I was in the third grade, I had a friend in my class named Chad. He had just moved to Park Ridge, Illinois, from the South. We hit it off immediately. We shared a common interest in baseball, and we quickly became best friends—absolutely inseparable. He became my "brother from another mother." But as time went on, my classmates and I noticed that our third-grade teacher loved Chad more than the rest of us. He was her favorite, her "pet"—not me. I wasn't used to this second-class treatment, and I didn't like it one bit. I had always been every teacher's pride and joy. Once I picked up on this, I was really mean to Chad. I would make fun of his once-endearing Southern accent. I would criticize the way he played second base. I made him cry several times. In my eight-year-old mind, Chad became the enemy. From that moment Chad became a Ninevite in my eyes.

At the end of the year, our elementary school always gave out an honor called the Citizenship Award. It was basically a certificate of recognition for the best student coupled with the best personality. In first and second grades I had been the recipient of that coveted award. On a hot June day, as we were all baking in the school gym, it came time for my teacher to announce the winner of the Citizenship Award. I was nervously hoping for another victory, another certificate of achievement to mount on my bedroom wall. But as I pretentiously stood up to claim my rightful prize, the teacher announced Chad as the winner of this year's award. I was devastated. I was irate. I became like Jonah, who in this story shows a very human response to God's kindness. We hate it when someone we don't like—or even worse, someone we loathe—receives favor from God.

Later, God asks a defiant Jonah, "Is it right for you to be angry?" (4:4). Jonah pouts like an overgrown infant and travels to the eastern part of the city in order to make a shelter and escape the heat. Like a chess player, he's waiting to see God's next move.

As I was reading this part of the story, I couldn't help but be reminded of that movie *Cast Away* in which Tom Hanks plays a FedEx employee who goes on a routine delivery flight only to have his plane crash in the middle of the ocean. He's left stranded on an island and, needing to be resourceful in every way, builds himself a shelter. Like most human beings, he eventually longs for some companionship. So he takes some of his own blood and makes a funny, smiling face on a volleyball, naming his new friend Wilson. Do you remember this?

Here, Jonah's not interested in companionship; he's content being left alone. Rather than caring about the destruction of the Ninevites, we see what's truly inside Jonah's heart. Jonah cares only about himself. He takes God's provision for granted. In verse 6, while Jonah is lounging on the mountainside where he can overlook the city, God provides him with a vine that grows over his head to ease his discomfort from the scorching Middle Eastern heat.

Isn't our God wonderful? He knew that Jonah's self-made shelter was lacking, so God lovingly sends him a gift. Jonah is like a little kid who receives a piece of his favorite candy. The text says, "Jonah was very happy about the plant." You would think that the words "Thank you, God" would fall out from Jonah's mouth. But that's not the case. Jonah fails to thank God for his provision. So verse 7 says that the next day God sends a little worm to eat up the vine that offered Jonah shade.

Jonah's outward reaction in verse 8 speaks volumes to what was really happening on the inside: "When the sun rose, God provided a scorching east wind, and the sun blazed on Jonah's head so that he grew faint. He wanted to die, and said, 'It would be better for me to die than to live.'"

Again God asks him, "Is it right for you to be angry about the plant?"

"'It is,' he said. 'And I'm so angry I wish I were dead'" (4:9). Jonah has become a very embittered man who has lost sight of what really matters. He cares only about himself.

Jonah, the prophet of God, cares about his physical comfort even more than he cares about lost souls. God makes this point when he explains in verses 10–11, "You have been concerned about this plant, though you did not tend it or make it grow. It sprang up overnight and died overnight. And should I not have concern for the great city of Nineveh, in which there are more than a hundred and twenty thousand people who cannot tell their right hand from their left—and also many animals?" God rebukes Jonah about the condition of his heart.

Jonathan Swift once revealed what's inside many Christians' hearts today when he said,

> We are God's chosen few;
> All others will be damned.
> There is no place in heaven for you,
> We can't have heaven crammed.

This common, unspoken attitude reveals Jonah's hardened heart. Jonah does not get what he wants, so he becomes angry with God. He goes after what he really wants, which is comfort. And he becomes so consumed with his own comfort that he could care less about the fact that many people will experience God's wrath and destruction.

What this story uncovers is that what we often care about is not what God cares about. Jonah cares more about his own physical comfort than lost souls who do not know God. Have we fallen into this trap? Do we care more about our material desires than reaching lost souls? Have we become too comfortable?

Much has been written about how Satan attacks Christians. Yes, he strikes Christians by encouraging doubt in who God is or by leading us to temptation. However, in recent years Satan's most effective weapon has been quite simple: encouraging a comfortable life.

Matt Slick, in his article "Are You Comfortable?" writes, "There is nothing wrong with being comfortable, unless that comfort makes us depend on God less and causes us to become complacent about the lost around us. . . . Are you so comfortable in your life that you aren't concerned about the lost, don't depend on God, tithe infrequently, and hardly seek God's face? . . . Remember, our life is not about our comforts. It is about loving God, loving others, and spreading the Word of God."

Jonah lost sight of what God cared about. He was consumed with his comfort and his hatred toward the Ninevites. Have we fallen into the devil's trap? Comfort creates apathy over time. We get comfortable doing nothing to advance God's kingdom. My prayer is that we will not live this lie of the devil. Jonah cared about the wrong things. What, then, are the right things to care about?

In the final two verses of chapter 4, God says to Jonah, "You have been concerned about this plant, though you did not tend it or make it grow. It sprang up overnight and died overnight. And should I not have concern for the great city of Nineveh, in which there are more than a hundred and twenty thousand people who cannot tell their right hand from their left—and also many animals?" (4:10–11).

God cares deeply for the salvation of people. While Jonah is ticked off because he knows how wretched the Ninevites are, God loves every person and we clearly see his heart in this passage. God desires for people everywhere to know him as the Lord of their lives. In 2 Peter 3:9, Peter writes, "The Lord is not slow in keeping his promise, as some understand slowness. Instead he is patient with you, not wanting anyone to perish, but everyone to come to repentance."

Do we have the heart of God today? Do we understand that our true purpose on this earth is to love and enjoy God and to share this message of God's love in Christ Jesus with everyone we meet? For those of us who do not yet know God, do you know that God is waiting patiently for you to acknowledge your need for him? God is waiting eagerly for you to respond to the good news that is found in his Son, Jesus Christ.

In Luke 15 there is a story about a wayward son. The younger of two sons takes his father's inheritance and wastes it on wild living. After some time living as a beggar, the son shamefully returns home to his father. What does the father do in response? He doesn't disown his child. He doesn't even rebuke him or punish him. Instead, Luke 15:20 states, "But while he was still a long way off, his father saw him and was filled with compassion for him; he ran to his son, threw his arms around him and kissed him."

This is a picture of the heart of God. God waits patiently for us to return to him. He loves us so much. He even runs to us after we've messed up our lives. This is the message of the gospel. God is love, and he loves us and wants us to be in loving relationship with him. Do we know this God?

At the end of Jonah's story we are left with a big unresolved question. God asks Jonah, "Should I not be concerned about that great city?" How does Jonah respond? We're not sure because we aren't given the rest of the details.

It seems that we are left with no call to action, but I believe there are applications that we can draw out. First, since God values lost souls, we should evangelize everyone. Do we have a heart of evangelism? When we see someone who doesn't know Jesus, do our hearts break for that person? Do we have concern for their eternal destiny? If we are a true God-fearing church, we are to share God's heart for the lost. If we lack this kind of heart or if we have become desensitized Christians, let's pray for God to rekindle that desire.

Second, may we love our enemies and care for their souls. No matter how good-natured we are, there are always some people we dislike or even disdain. They may not be enemies per se, but our bodies tell us when that person is in the room because our blood pressure rises and our faces burn up with a fiery red glow.

Jonah clearly lacked love for his enemies, yet Jesus tells us that we are to love our enemies and pray for those who persecute us. If you are having a tough time loving someone, pray that God would change your heart. So many times we pray for God to change the other person. Today God calls us to change and to love the unlovable. This is the heart of someone who follows Jesus Christ: we love our enemies and pray for those who do us wrong. Something that Jonah forgot to remember is that Christians care about what God cares about.

Christians care about what God cares about. God cares about the lost. God cares about the poor. God cares about the widows and orphans of this world. God cares about those who are dying of malaria and AIDS. God cares about those in the inner city who do not know when their next meal is coming. God cares about injustice. God cares about racism and prejudice. God cares about his people, every single one of them. The question is, do we care about what God cares about?

In Billy Graham's autobiography *Just As I Am*, he writes toward the end of the book, "One thing will not change: God's love for humanity and His desire to see men and women yield their lives to Him and come to know Him in a personal way. The human spirit is never satisfied in a lasting way by anything less than God. We were made for Him."

What are we living for here on this earth? What do we care about? Jonah forgot that God's people care about what God cares about. My prayer is that we will live only for what God cares about. It is only then that we will experience the abundant life that God intended for us. Christians care about what God cares about.

Commentary

When you think of the book of Jonah, what do you think about? Large fish or a wet prophet? Matt Kim uses all four chapters of Jonah to get his message across. One value of a narrative approach is that you can give all kinds of information that the audience doesn't hear as a lecture. He has told us Nineveh had one hundred twenty thousand people, and the people were hard and callous. When Nineveh repented, which would have been unthinkable to most people in the ancient world, they changed their lives. Kim talks about Nineveh repenting and then about Jonah being angry at God's forgiveness. So the question is, Why is Jonah angry because God is good? In answering that question, Kim doesn't simply give us biblical admonition. He tells us a story. Our tendency is to say, "those are terrible people." But in telling us a story about himself, he is telling us that Jonah's heart is very much like our own.

Interview

How do you prepare to preach?

During my time as a senior pastor, I typically began sermon preparation on Tuesday. I began my preparation each week by reading the Scripture text a number of times to get a handle on what the author was saying. Then I would try to translate the passage into English from the original languages and do word studies. On Wednesday I would work on getting the central idea of the passage and come up with the outline of the sermon. On Thursday and Friday I would write out my manuscript and fill in the outline with content and illustrations. On Saturday night I would read over the manuscript three times before going to sleep. I would wake up on Sunday morning and rehearse the sermon twice out loud.

Do you use a sermon calendar?

In the pastorate, I created a sermon calendar at least six months in advance. At best, I would prepare a calendar for twelve months ahead of time. In between sermon series I took one of my "off weeks" when I wasn't preaching and used that time to plan out the next set of sermons.

How do you come up with a sermon series? Why "Men of the Old Testament"?

My goal was to help the congregation know God's Word. I went into a church context that didn't know their Bibles. One year I decided to spend the entire year preaching through the Old Testament by giving an overview of one book each Sunday. The next year I preached on each book of the New Testament each Sunday. It was a challenge to try to condense what I thought was the big idea of each book of the Bible, but I believe God accomplished something wonderful by giving the church a better grasp of the central ideas of the Bible.

I chose to do two different series one summer, going through various Bible characters and their successes and failures. So I decided to do a sermon series on "Men of the Old Testament" and a second series on "Women of the Old Testament."

You have a clear central idea. How often do you typically repeat your central idea? Why do you think it's important to repeat it?

Every sermon is different in terms of how often I feel it is necessary to repeat the big idea. Usually, I try to repeat the idea at least three times. But in an inductive type of sermon, for example, I will simply state the central idea only once at the conclusion of the sermon. The central idea will be my final sentence for listeners to take home with them.

What were the challenges in preaching this text? What are the challenges in preaching an Old Testament prophet?

This sermon was one of the sermons from the "Men of the Old Testament" series. My attempt was to condense four chapters of material in the book of Jonah into one message. One of the challenges was figuring out which details to include about the historical context of Jonah's day. Another challenging aspect of this particular sermon was preaching a familiar story in a new way. Instead of focusing on the fish, I spent most of the sermon targeting the root problem, which was the condition of Jonah's heart versus the heart of God.

Old Testament prophetical books are difficult to preach because as we read through them, each chapter appears to be saying the same thing. It can become quite repetitive. God is calling the nations to repent and come back to him. How do we preach themes of repentance and redemption from chapter to chapter? The key, I believe, is to focus on the central idea of each text and offer variety through our stories, illustrations, and creativity.

Who was your audience? Please describe your church setting.

This sermon was preached to the congregation that I served as senior pastor in Denver, Colorado. It consisted of primarily second-generation Asian Americans and also some Caucasians. Our church ranged quite broadly with respect to spiritual life. We had nonbelievers, young believers, and mature believers.

If your congregation said one thing about your preaching, what would you want it to be?

I hope they would say that in every sermon I preached, God was glorified and they encountered him in a real and lasting way.

What advice would you give to a young preacher?

One of the things that I learned as a younger preacher is that it takes time to develop a preaching voice and know who you are as a preacher. It is very easy to mimic your favorite preacher, but the sermons will not be authentic. It took about two full years of preaching before I became comfortable in my own skin.

A second word of advice that I would offer a young preacher would be to spend quality time in sermon preparation. We're not promised fifteen to twenty hours of solitude per week at the church office, but we can make a concerted effort to create boundaries so that we are able to give proper time and attention to the important task of preaching God's Word.

Do you use notes? Why or why not?

In the beginning of my preaching ministry I used notes because I was nervous. But after the first year I didn't bring notes up with me to the pulpit because they eventually became a distraction in terms of sermon delivery. The irony is that we tend to think that we'll be freer when using notes, but it's actually the opposite. When you ask preachers who use notes or a manuscript how often they look down, most will tell you a number far less than what actually takes place. I found that as long as I had a clear central idea, a clear outline, and clear illustrations, I did not need to use notes because of the sermon's clarity. Our goal in preaching is to be crystal clear.

Do you collect illustrations? Tell me about the importance of illustrations.

I have a computer file where I have created various thematic categories for illustrations. When I find helpful illustrations from the newspaper, magazine articles, or stories, I will put them into one of the computer files.

Without illustrations, sermons become flat and one-dimensional. It's difficult to listen to preachers who don't illustrate well or often enough during the course of a sermon. Illustrations are extremely important to help the listener connect his or her experiences with the Bible. As preachers, we want our listeners to identify with the Bible and to be changed by God's Word rather than have them think that the Bible is irrelevant.

How do you determine sermon form?

The form of the sermon is usually but not always dictated by the flow of the Scripture text. In many sermons from New Testament epistles, we find that the sermonic form is deductive. On the other hand, narrative sermons are often inductive in their shape. I shape the sermon based on the genre of the Scripture text and what I believe makes most sense in conveying the main idea to the congregation.

You talk about application in your sermon: "It seems that we are left with no call to action, but I believe there are applications that we can draw out." What was the difficulty in applying this sermon?

Applying the text can be difficult in any sermon. How many times have we heard the preacher just say, "Go home and pray about it"? Prayer is significant, but it's not the application of every passage. In this sermon, the challenge with respect to application was helping my listeners see that in every Christian there is a tendency to have a heart like Jonah's, which was far from the heart of God. My goal was to help them identify with Jonah and evaluate their spiritual condition.

The applications that I drew from this text were twofold. First, God wants his people to evangelize and bring the story of forgiveness and redemption to the world. Second, we are to love our enemies. Jonah's hatred for the Ninevites caused him to be blind to God's redemptive plan. God calls us to love those with whom we can't find common ground.

Tell about your use of media from the pulpit.

In various sermons I have used PowerPoint presentations, shown video clips, or played Christian songs. Media can be a valuable tool in preaching as long as it is appropriate and seamless in its delivery. Preachers today sometimes overuse media and it isn't carefully thought out. We need to make sure that media isn't simply for entertainment value or to occupy time, but that it enhances our communication and our sermon.

How would you describe expository preaching in your own words?

Expository preaching is communicating God's Word boldly, clearly, and tangibly for the purpose of life transformation in the preacher and in the listeners.

11

Can God Be Both Just and Loving?

Topical

CHRIS DOLSON

R ecently a friend of mine invited me to his place of business to see how things work. I jumped at the opportunity. My friend's name is John and he is the editor of the *Wisconsin State Journal* (*WSJ*). Most of us are pretty familiar with the *WSJ*. Many of us start out our day by reading either the online or print version. We know where the *WSJ* building is located downtown; we've probably driven past it hundreds of times. I certainly know where the building is, and I was thrilled to drive down there and have the editor give me a tour.

On our tour we walked past lots of desks with people looking at computer screens and talking on the phone. It was a very busy place. They have a huge print and distribution area toward the back of the building—it's like a separate building in and of itself. We were there in the afternoon when it was quiet, but in the evening the presses get going as the shipments start to leave the building. Probably the highlight of the tour was when John let me sit in on their "page one" meeting. This is where all the editors and key news journalists sit around a table and make final decisions about the placement of the stories for the next day's page one, which is printed shortly after the meeting. I was impressed with how professional everyone was and how short the meeting was.

A funny thing happened at the end of the afternoon as John escorted me to the door after my tour. He *apologized* and told me that he really isn't the

Chris Dolson is senior pastor of Blackhawk Church, a multisite, multivenue church of four thousand in Middleton, Wisconsin. Chris preaches four to five times per weekend.

best tour guide. He told me that, even as the editor of the paper, there is a lot about the paper and the building that he doesn't know. He has a lot to learn.

I was there just a couple of hours, but I learned a ton about the newspaper business. I thought I knew something about the paper that is so familiar to me and so much a part of my life, but I really didn't know much about what goes on at the *WSJ* until that tour. And in reality, on that tour I just scratched the surface about how to run a newspaper in today's media-frenzied world.

The reason I'm telling that story is that I kind of feel like John when I stand up here and talk about God. It's like I'm taking you on a tour of something that we all believe we're pretty familiar with. We talk about God a lot. We mention his name, pray to him, sing songs to him and about him. It's like I'm taking you inside a building that we have driven by hundreds of times. We think we know what goes on inside the building, but when we take a tour we learn that we really didn't know that much and the tour just scratches the surface. I talk to you about God a lot, but these talks barely scratch the surface of who our God actually is.

One more thing: like John, I don't think I'm the best tour guide. I am still learning and have lots to learn. There is an awful lot about God that I don't understand or can't fathom. I'm really in over my head when I stand up here and talk about God.

The problem gets even worse because we live in a world that is all about a "designer god"—that is, we live in a world where people like to design their own god. Whatever you think is important, that is what you put into the design of your god.

It's like that store in the mall called "Build-A-Bear Workshop." You go into the store and pick out a toy bear that you like, and then you stuff it and dress it just the way you want. You literally "build a bear." It's a great father-daughter date.

Many of us do the same thing with God. We kind of "Build-A-God." It works in our minds like this:

- Let's say in your mind that the most important thing about God is that he is powerful. Then as you build your God, *power wins*.
- Let's say in your mind that the most important thing about God is that he is loving. Then as you build your God, *love wins*. If someone comes up to you and says that God will someday judge a person for their actions, you say, "My God wouldn't do that; he would never

judge anyone. He is a loving God." If someone talks about hell, you say, "No—there is no hell because love wins."

- Let's say that in your mind God's wrath and judgment are the most important things. Then as you build your God, *judgment wins*. When someone says, "God might be gracious to a person," you'd reply, "My God wouldn't do that. He can't have anything to do with disobedience; he is a God of judgment."

So even though I'm not the best tour guide and we live in a world of "designer gods," today I want to take us on a tour. On this tour I want to talk about two things that are true about God but are often hard to put together at the same time: God is loving and God is just.

Love and *justice* are two words that we are pretty familiar with; we toss those words around a lot. Just Google either word and you'll get tons of entries (*love*—over 7 billion results; *justice*—over 550 million results). When these words are applied to God in the Bible, there are books and articles written that would take us years to go through. But don't worry, today's tour will be brief. This is what we'll see on the tour:

- God is a God of love. What does that mean and what does that not mean?
- God is a God of justice. What does that mean and what does that not mean?
- These two things taken together create what is perceived to be a problem: How can God be both loving and just at the same time? This is only a perceived problem to us; it has never been a problem to God. That becomes clear when we look to the cross. God is both loving and just at the same time, and the cross makes that clear.

Let's start our tour. God is loving.

The LORD is just in all his actions, and exhibits love in all he does. (Ps. 145:17 NET)

God is love. (1 John 4:16)

Finally, brothers and sisters, rejoice! Strive for full restoration, encourage one another, be of one mind, live in peace. And the *God of love* and peace will be with you. (2 Cor. 13:11, emphasis added)

The Greek word used here for "love" is *agape*. Agape love is described for us in the famous passage of 1 Corinthians 13:4–8.

> Love is patient, love is kind. It does not envy, it does not boast, it is not proud. It does not dishonor others, it is not self-seeking, it is not easily angered, it keeps no record of wrongs. Love does not delight in evil but rejoices with the truth. It always protects, always trusts, always hopes, always perseveres. Love never fails.

We might define agape love in this way: Agape love acts for the well-being of another regardless of how he or she responds to me. In other words, agape love makes *no demands* on the person loved.

Agape love is giving. Agape love is not demanding. Agape love doesn't demand the person must change but loves that person just the way he or she is. It does not keep a record of wrongs that the person has done.

Agape is not the same as *eros*, which is another Greek word for love. Eros is about me, agape is about you. Eros is self-fulfilling, agape is self-sacrificing.

> Eros is the desire to possess and to enjoy; agape is the willingness to serve without reservations. . . . Agape is a gift love whereas eros is a need love. Eros springs from a deficiency that must be satisfied. Agape is the overflowing abundance of divine grace.
>
> Donald Bloesch (*God the Almighty*, p. 146)

God is love and he loves everything, with one huge exception: God does not love evil. Why? Because the very essence of evil is to resist, reject, and refuse the love of God. Evil is essentially rebellion against God. Evil wrecks what God says is good.

Evil causes God to react. He sees something that is not right and he wants to do something about it. This comes from the fact that God is a God of justice. When God sees a wreck he reacts to the wreck. He does that because he is a God of justice.

We are moving along on our tour. There are many verses in the Bible that speak of God's justice.

> The Lord is just in all his actions, and exhibits love in all he does. (Ps. 145:17 NET)

He is the Rock, his works are perfect,
    and all his ways are just.
A faithful God who does no wrong,
    upright and just is he. (Deut. 32:4)

Trust me, there are other verses in the Bible that say God is just.

What is justice? Justice is about setting things right. You see something
that is not right and you want to do something about it. When things are
out of place, it is the role of justice to put the pieces back together. Justice
says, "No, that's not right"—and then it wants to fix the mess.

Watch this video.

[Show a YouTube video of an Ally Bank commercial showing a man
who is being unfair to one girl concerning the meaning of the word *pony*.
http://www.youtube.com/watch?v=7qb0vquRcys]

There is something in all of us that says, "That's not fair! That's not
right!" Creating that feeling of dissonance inside of each one of us is what
that commercial is all about. They are hoping people will react against the
unjust practices of their own banks and do something about that (that is,
choose *their* bank). It is an ingenious advertisement that plays on the sense
of right and wrong built into all of us. The commercial is an illustration
of injustice. The first little girl doesn't *deserve* to be treated that way. The
first little girl *deserves* to be treated the same way as the other little girl.

Justice is about what you deserve. In justice you get what you *deserve*.

Unlike agape love, justice makes demands and cries out for change.
Justice says, "That's not right." Justice makes demands of situations that
need to be made right. God has that sense in a big way. When God sees
something is wrong, his attribute of justice causes him to react. God's
reaction to evil is his wrath. His wrath is not the opposite of his love but
is a function of it.

Frederick Bruner puts it like this in his book *Matthew* (p. 1:92): "[Wrath]
is the love of God in friction with the reality of injustice. . . . God's wrath
does not contradict God's love; it proves it. *A love that pampers injustice
is not lovable.*" Imagine going back to the man in the pony commercial
and saying, "That's okay, you go ahead and keep treating the girl that way.
I'll just overlook it." That would be unloving and unjust.

This brings us to the next stop on our tour, to what *seems to us* like a big problem: How can God be both loving and just at the same time? Do you see the tension? Agape (love) makes *no demands* of people, but justice *makes demands*. Justice says, "That's not right! Fix it." That is very demanding.

How can God make no demands and then make demands at the same time? He wants to love sinful people but he can't turn his back on our sin. How can he show us justice without compromising his love? How can he love us without compromising his justice?

In the Bible we see that these two tensions are placed side by side. Sometimes we don't even notice it, especially when we read familiar passages like John 3:16.

> For God so loved the world that he gave his one and only Son, that whoever believes in him shall not perish but have eternal life. For God did not send his Son into the world to condemn the world, but to save the world through him. Whoever believes in him is not condemned, but whoever does not believe stands condemned already because they have not believed in the name of God's one and only Son. (John 3:16–18)

(Note: Immediately after reading 3:16 ask, "Why would anyone be in danger of perishing if God is a loving God?" The answer is that God is both loving and just.)

If you have a Bible that has red letters for the words of Jesus, I think that the right interpretation is that the words in 3:16 are in black and not red. Jesus is not speaking. John, the writer, is explaining to the reader what Jesus is doing at his first coming (Advent). He is writing after Jesus has come and died—notice the past tense in 3:16 ("he *gave* his one and only Son"). Jesus's first coming was not about bringing judgment; rather it was about bringing salvation. This time Jesus didn't come to judge the world, he came to save the world.

The word *love* is obvious in verse 16, but the word *justice* is not. However, the words that are translated "condemned" and "verdict" in the subsequent verses all translate the Greek word group that also means "justice and judgment." John is explaining what Jesus is doing at his first coming (Advent): He came to save the world. But Jesus is also the judge. He will come again, and then he will come as the Judge.

Moreover, the Father judges no one, but has entrusted all judgment to the Son, that all may honor the Son just as they honor the Father. Whoever does not honor the Son does not honor the Father, who sent him. Very truly I tell you, whoever hears my word and believes him who sent me has eternal life and will not be judged but has crossed over from death to life. Very truly I tell you, a time is coming and has now come when the dead will hear the voice of the Son of God and those who hear will live. For as the Father has life in himself, so he has granted the Son also to have life in himself. And he has given him authority to judge because he is the Son of Man. (John 5:22–27)

The cross represents a wonderful paradox; two things were happening at the same time on the cross. God was loving the world and judging the world all at the same time. The Judge was being judged for us. God was pouring out his anger against sin and injustice onto his Son. He himself absorbed this judgment in the person of his Son because he is a loving God.

Sometimes as Christ-followers we can misrepresent what is happening on the cross. Sometimes we make it sound like God sent Christ to protect us from an angry God. Jesus had to die on a cross in order to placate an angry God. Jesus loves us while God is angry at us. This makes God an opponent and an adversary, and Jesus is our ally.

But this is not what John 3:16 says: "For *God* so loved the world." The work of Christ is the work of God. The cross of Christ is God at work. God is saving the world. God is not our adversary; he is extending himself into the condition of our humanity and bringing about our salvation.

Why is this concept important? It shows that God himself is on our side. He did not send a messenger, Jesus, to do his dirty work. Jesus is God. God came himself.

All this is from God, who reconciled us to himself through Christ and gave us the ministry of reconciliation: that God was reconciling the world to himself in Christ, not counting people's sins against them. (2 Cor. 5:18–19)

The cross is not the work of Christ against God and for us. The cross is the work of God for us. Jesus didn't come to the world to change God's mind toward us but to express the mind of God.

The work of the cross is the work of God. The Judge is judged for us.

One final thing before our tour is over: Some of us have heard a message like this before, but for whatever reason we have never placed our faith in

Christ. Look at John 5:24 again. That verse helps us to picture something like a line between death and life. Those who have believed cross over that line to eternal life and will not be judged! Do you see that?

If I were to place a line up here on the platform—on one side it would represent belief in Christ and on the other side it would represent unbelief—where would you stand?

I want to say this as clearly and as lovingly as possible. If you have not believed in Jesus, you are in danger of perishing! Something could happen to you today as you leave this building, and you would perish—you would spend an eternity apart from God.

Sometimes I hear people say things like this:

Cancer is the worst thing that could happen to a person.
Losing a child is the worst thing that could happen to a person.
Divorce is the worst thing that could happen to a person.
Losing your career is the worst thing that could happen to a person.

Those are all horrible things, but let's be clear: They are not the absolute worst thing that could happen to a person. Perishing apart from Christ is the worst possible thing that could happen to a person.

You would perish, not because God is *not* loving but precisely because he *is* loving. He cannot, as a loving God, pamper and tolerate injustice or evil. If you are on the unbelief side of the line, you are bearing your evil and your injustice apart from Christ, and he will judge you.

For the love of God I appeal to you: Place your faith in Christ. Step over that line.

(Close in prayer, inviting people to place their faith in Christ.)

Commentary

Chris Dolson preaches an evangelistic sermon that is theologically solid but not expository. He sets up a scenario in which he's invited by the editor of the *Wisconsin State Journal* to visit the newspaper's building downtown. He knew about the paper, but he didn't know about the building. John, the editor, is showing him around but he comments that he doesn't think he is the best guide. He says he is still learning and that there is a lot to learn. Dolson takes that phrase and applies it to himself and his knowledge of God.

There are two things about God that are laid out. God is just and God is loving. That apparent contradiction is at the heart of the sermon. Dolson shows how God can be both loving and just and does so in a down-to-earth, practical sort of way. The questions at the end of the sermon stand out because they are very different than the others. He begins his preparation for a Sunday six months out. He doesn't prepare a sermon by himself but has a whole team of people who work with him. It introduces a different quality of message that preachers might want to consider. How you prepare is as important as what you prepare.

Interview

How do you go about preparing a sermon?

I'm looking for two things: (1) What's the text saying? and (2) What will I say about that? Discovering what the text is saying involves an enormous amount of study.

When do you prepare for Sunday?

Usually six months out.

And part of your sermon preparation involves meeting regularly with a team?

It's a huge process. There are lots of teams, so it's a matter of working with all kinds of folks. It starts with a huge group, a kind of macro oversight group that's made up of key people on my staff. I trust them a lot in terms of what we are going to be preaching. That team includes myself, another key leader, a speaker from the speaking team, and another strategic leadership team member. My wife is part of that team. She doesn't work for us, but she has a good sense of things. I trust her a lot. It's a very small group of people, and these people are core.

Next, we gather a think tank group. Eventually we get to a creative arts planning team (CAP).

By that time I've prepared preliminary notes. All speakers are required to write one page (max) of preliminary notes. At the top of the page is the date and the text, followed by the purpose of the message and the main idea. Then the notes must include a couple of sentences describing what the sermon is going to be about. The description might say, "This is a big message on grace" or "This is an evangelistic message." The speaker needs to give enough information so that people who are not familiar with the passage will be able to discuss how to approach the topic creatively. That's the CAP team, and they get together and they just fire ideas, like "Let's get the donkeys."

Then comes a decision-making group. The decision team gets together and says, "No. No donkeys. Donkeys are stupid." We knock out things. We come up with video ideas. All of this is behind the sermon preparation. It's all driven by what the speaker is going to say.

Can you give us a specific example of how the creative process contributes to the sermon?

Habakkuk is in a conversation with God. He's complaining to God and God responds to him and he says something like, "It doesn't matter if I have sheep in the pen or if there are no cattle. It doesn't matter. I will trust you." So this message is about faith. How do we trust God in really difficult times, when the world's falling apart? Obviously we have people whose worlds are falling apart. We found one of those people. She's a cancer victim. She's dying. She can hardly speak because she has so many canker sores in her mouth. Our video production team got behind that. We interviewed her. The team recorded the interview and it was powerful. We placed it at the end of the sermon. In the conclusion of the message I said, "Habakkuk was struggling with God. He was a person of faith. We have a woman named Betty in our congregation. She's a person of faith. Here is her story." Then I stepped down and—*boom*. It's a punch in the gut. In order to get there we probably started this whole process six months ago. Six months ago I knew we were going to do Habakkuk, so I had preliminary notes and in the preliminary meetings we knew this would be a great story.

It sounds like you really utilize technology.

Absolutely. We're a big church. We have lots of people here. Many of them are creative artists.

How long does it take to prepare a sermon?

If you're talking about the study part, thirty to forty hours. In terms of the sermon and what I'm going to say that would relate to people, it's not thirty hours in a week. It's scattered over months.

There's something we have found here that really is helpful, and I've found it to be unique. All of our speakers have to be what we call "two weeks out." I heard about that years ago, and when I made that switch it was great. You have to be disciplined enough to do it yourself. The thing that gets speakers going is that you have the deadline. If you're looking at a calendar right now, the 29th was this past Sunday. My deadline for the 29th would be the 17th. I had to have everything finished by then. We've been doing it for years, and the reason you can do it is because you have a team of people who get guns and sharp knives after you if you don't do it.

That's the deadline, two weeks out. Then I put the message away because I'm working on another thing two weeks out. In fact, if you came up to me on July 27th and asked me what I was preaching on Sunday, I might draw a blank. I can't remember what I'm preaching this Sunday, but on Saturday the 28th at two or three in the afternoon I review my planning notes, which are almost a full manuscript. Then I spend eight hours on Saturday completing the manuscript. I already have an almost-full manuscript in my planning notes, so it's just a matter of cutting and pasting. But while I'm doing that I'm getting it back into my mind again. It's coming back, and then on Sunday morning I'm up at five and working on it again. Since I've already done all that work, it comes right back.

Why do the additional work of the manuscript when you already have the planning notes?

Haddon told me to write a full manuscript. I didn't do it for a long time, but he embarrassed me in class and said, "Well, Chris doesn't do that." So then I started to do it, and it really made a big difference.

What was the difference?

It's the whole idea of wordsmithing. You think more about wording. I require all my speakers to write a manuscript.

Do you preach with notes?

I'm pretty note-less. Most people would say I don't use notes, but I do have sticky notes in my Bible. They're hidden around the text in my Bible so nobody sees them. If I have a screaming child or something happens where I get lost, I need something that reminds me where I'm going. Sticky notes are made for preachers. I just love them. I make little notes next to the text. I have a color-coding system. Blue means PowerPoint or look to the screen.

How did you come to preach this sermon?

It's part of a larger series that we were doing. We began with a series called "American Idols," things that we give ultimate value to in our culture. The contrast to that series is "Behold Your God." Everything launched off of the Isaiah 40 passage. It was a theme passage throughout "American Idols" and "Behold Your God." In this series the question we asked was "What prevents us from following?"

We have a document that states what this series is about and why we are doing it. My question is "What prevents us from reordering our lives, following Jesus, obeying Jesus's teaching?" We have given our allegiance to other gods. We follow other gods. We don't actually understand the character of our true God, and we harbor deep suspicions about who he is. We misunderstand him. We don't trust him. So the series answers the question "What is our God like?" One of the messages is "Our God Is Incomprehensible." Another is titled "God Is Powerful and Good." This message is about God's justice and love. He's both of these things, and that creates a problem. We took things that people would have problems with.

What are the challenges in preaching a topical sermon?

You run like a mad dog away from the text. Haddon talks about wild stallions. You get on them and they run away. He warns against those stallions because they run far away and get lost and you have to harness them. A topical message moves you away from the text. You have one or two texts, and they launch an idea and you get really far away from any biblical concept.

How do you rein that in?

It's difficult. Hopefully I'm just trying to be fair to what's happening. I used a long illustration in the introduction about how the editor of a newspaper took us through his workplace and in the end he says, "I still have a lot to learn about the newspaper business." He's the editor! Well, in this sermon I talk about God and how there's so much to say. So here are a few verses that say God is loving and here are a few that say God is just. This creates a problem for most people. How do we solve that problem? I just grabbed a few verses that say God is loving and God is just and whip them right out of context, but I think in this sermon most people say, "Okay, I know, I trust you. The Bible probably does tell us he's loving and just, but how do you put them together, that's the problem."

Tell me about the audience for this sermon.

We've got about four thousand attendees at multiple venues. Our largest room holds about seven hundred. I have about seven hundred or eight hundred people in front of me when I preach, so we record the message and it's taken to the other room. We burn disks and it's taken to other venues.

How would you describe expository preaching in your own words?

The message that people hear is driven by what the biblical author is saying, so the audience would say, "That makes a lot of sense. I understand what you're saying." And if the biblical author was in the audience he'd say, "Yeah, that's what I meant."

What are you trying to accomplish in an introduction?

It has to answer the questions everybody is thinking: Why should I listen to what you're going to say? Why is this interesting? How is this going to touch my life in some way? People are busy, they don't have time, their lives are messed up, and we all need to hear a word from God. They want to know: What are you going to say to me today?

What advice would you give to a young preacher? What encouragement would you give to a more seasoned preacher?

To young preachers, they need to find their own voices.

Most of the young people I train are trying to do too much in a talk. They have four points that could probably be broken into four sermons. Don't do too much. Know your sermon's purpose. What I learned from Haddon is that the purpose drives the preparation.

As to encouragement for seasoned preachers, don't be afraid of fifteen- and sixteen-year-olds. Don't try to preach to their parents. Preach to them.

If I can hit the seventeen-year-old, that's my target audience. I'm shooting for the sixteen-year-old. That's my target. I appreciate the fact that people are in their thirties and forties, but I'm trying to hit the seventeen-year-old. As far as I'm concerned, I'm hitting the junior and senior high school students. Their brains are fully developed and there's nothing in them. I'm in a university context, and graduate students have got so much stuff in their brains, you're lucky if you can get them at all. But the seventeen-year-olds, I don't want their minds to wander. I want them to focus. How can I help them focus? I got that from Earl Palmer years ago and it really helped me a lot.

You give a call to cross the line in the conclusion. Is that typical in your conclusions?

No, it's atypical for me.

Did that have to do with the purpose for that week?

The written purpose is, *To help the audience see how the justice and love of God come together at the cross.* The main idea is, *The cross of Christ demonstrates the love and justice of God.* The purpose here is a little squishy. I'm moving toward the cross and I went to a decision and I had this big circle on the board where I was drawing two things. They're opposite and I put the cross in the center that brings these two things together. It's not a problem for God. It's solved at the cross. Then I have these verses. I put a mark on the inside of the line and on the outside and I ask, "Where are you?" I challenge people and I say, "You could perish. Anyone on the outside of this line is going to perish." It's heavy, heavy language, and I try to be as nice as I can, but I challenge people to place their trust in the cross.

I would say this is an evangelistic topical message, although it felt more like an interesting theological discussion. I really wanted to help people trust Christ, and a number of people came to faith through this talk. We heard stories of people who said they crossed the line. People have said, "Remember the Sunday you put the thing up? I crossed the line."

Tell me about your use of illustrations. Do you collect them?

I don't collect them. Spending time looking for illustrations is time consuming. I've got thousands of 3x5 cards. When I went to computer world in the 1990s I said, "I'm going to have to transfer these, but no way. There are too many of them." So every once in a while, when I'm really desperate, I'll go to my 3x5 cards. Sometimes I'll find stuff, but most of the time I don't.